Daniel E. Tanzo

How you get to the stream matters not; as long as you take a first sip, something is possible.

Tanzoism # 3

Silk

She is

Poetry by
Daniel E. Tanzo

Daniel E. Tanzo

Silk She Is

Poetry by Daniel E. Tanzo

ISBN: 978-1495357701

WPaD Fundraiser Edition, Paperback

Copyright © 2014 Daniel E. Tanzo and WPaD Publications

This intellectual property has been published with author's permission for the purpose of charity fundraising.

Rights to this edition in all media, physical and digital, are reserved by the publisher, WPaD Publications.

Proceeds from sale of this book will be donated to the American Cancer Society, in accordance with Mr. Tanzo's wishes.

Silk She Is

About the Author:

Raised in Antioch, California, Daniel E. Tanzo is a US Army veteran and former construction company owner and laborer. A self-proclaimed poet/warrior, he began his exploration to his path in 1998. Always an avid reader and lover of words, he was introduced to Rumi, Hafiz, Cohelo and Borges, igniting his own poetry. He has spoken in front of various audiences, including the San Francisco World Conference on the Enneagram. He studied alchemy through the written word at a Bay area based mystery school. A new and recent yoga student, he has continued to write poetry and pursue his spiritual path while being caregiver to his mother after her debilitating stroke. After losing his mother to cancer, he was himself diagnosed with cancer shortly afterward.

This book was compiled, at Daniel's request, by a friend who is a fellow writer and admirer of his work. His unique perspective on life and love is expressed with a divine eloquence that catches the reader by surprise if said reader is familiar with only the man's rough exterior. The title, *Silk She Is*, was chosen by Dan, but the poem that is the namesake for this book is missing. Dan tried to retrieve it from his files because he wanted it in the book, but we ran out of time. The cover design is based on the image he described, and when he saw it, he said it was "perfect".

"I was raised to be a "Man" by a father, uncles and various male role models, coaches etc. This meant, in my particular Bay Area industrial town, don't cry, never back down from a fight, and all the rest of those peculiar aspects that were passed on and down to us young males. I thoroughly embraced these as biblical writ: I was in the armed forces, where of course this was further enhanced, and became a bouncer at a local watering hole. I have pulled my own tooth and even stitched myself up with an actual needle and thread. So I guess I qualify as to these male standards."

~ Daniel E. Tanzo ~

During the toughest battle of his life, Dan fought like a bear, never backing down for a minute. He will forever be loved and missed by friends worldwide. This book is his legacy; and Dan has asked that the proceeds be donated to cancer research.

'Grizz' is now free to roam the afterlife, expressing his poetic wisdom amongst the stars.

Daniel E. Tanzo

When you're invited to life, scream,
"HELL, YEAH!" and go,
but remember to bring a dish or a jug of wine
to share, don'tcha know.

Tanzoism # 8

Island of Misfits

Here's to the crazy ones.

The misfits.

The rebels.

The troublemakers.

The round pegs in the square holes.

The ones who see things differently.

They're not fond of rules.

And they have no respect for the status quo.

You can praise them, disagree with them, quote them,

disbelieve them, glorify or vilify them.

About the only thing you can't do is ignore them.

Because they change things

Daniel E. Tanzo

Remove the filtered lenses of others; see with the filter of your heart's experience.

Tanzoism # 15

Silk She Is

Pirate Latitudes

Too often I sat,

like a sailor on a battleship in its harbor,

playing it safe,

displaying my guns

while I watched smaller ships sail into the seas.

You know, the ones so different from me.

Content to bask in the glory

unchallenging thoughts

patting each other like dogs

on old ladies' laps.

Look how alike and shiny we are,

Navigate by land and only what's seen.

Those others they look to the stars,

and traverse, what I can't tell,

I preferred to live in my small tiny cell,

bolstered by the shared certitude of ignorance

espousing parrot platitudes

then I jumped ship

for

pirate latitudes

Daniel E. Tanzo

Oft times it's easier to run to the old familiar; it's safe and predictable, and easily controlled.

Venturing out to the unknown takes willingness to be wrong, and risks the ego and the heart.

That's the measure of a warrior.

Tanzoism # 41

Silk She Is

Bottom of Form

Alpha to omega
been there done that
more than twice
Shape shifting shaman
who willingly paid the price
Scars at the throat
remnants of the first death match
Charnal house to bawdy house
loving whores and killing floors
It's what I did and where I thrived

I don't propose to change other people's minds; that's their job. I just choose to speak mine.

Tanzoism # 5

Silk She Is

There can be only one;

it's just the way I'm made,

I have not the guile,

nor the will, to, travel with parades.

An entourage of homage,

I need just the one, whose laughter,

is my song of blessing.

In her banter and wit,

names me Don Juan

full of shit.

There can be no other.

Other than you.

'tis true.

Daniel E. Tanzo

Mists

I seek the Mists of Love,
Tendrils, wrapped like vines.
Coveting the Unspoken
Like Red Wine Bathing

Silk She Is

I awaken because of you
I smile laugh and weep with you
your sorrows are mine.
Your triumphs lift me.
The moon a beacon
messenger to and from you,
the hills?
your body and clefts
all blatant reminders of you
An ancient rythimcal dance.
A duet of quickening passions,
breathless friction,
breathful sighs.
Your joy beckons mine
and mine yours.

Daniel E. Tanzo

        ℰarly to bed
And surprise at sunrise,
the slow awakening,
of sibilant thighs
and moanful sighs
The scent of night past
on her skin,
once more we begin.

Silk She Is

Seduction of a Temptress

You are like the grass in the meadows
swaying in breezes
to the song of the wind
that rustles the trees.
The first sweet taste
of pomegranate
trickling across my tongue.
To traverse you properly
I need no compass,
your sighs guide me
unerringly toward
your cathedral where I
as humble supplicant
worship in ecstatic wonderment
Drinking from the baptismal font

Daniel E. Tanzo

Aphrodite's Lament

My envy is alive
It grows and gnaws
in my thoughts
it harkens my soul
to mournful lamentation.
I curse the clouds and rain,
which pass over and caress
Her with light touch.

I am Aphrodite, who
till now,
was viewed and approached
only with Awe and Reverence
by those in love with Love.
I who find myself supplanted
By the one He calls She!

Silk She Is

No equal had I known
TILL NOW!
To be surpassed by mere Mortal!
Never I cried
Yet it is her name
He mutters in his slumber

Whose smile and gaze he craves
I know this, as my Brother Morpheus
delights in recounting His dreams
of her to me.

My strong lamed Hephestus
Who conquered Aries
Apollo and more for me
Seeks and Sees
Now alone
This, this Gypsy
This SHE.

Blood for Pens

Red Ribbons of proof to a disbelieving mind
Subtleties lost to the hordes of mundane drones
whose only desire is the right car and home.

We are the werewolves,
The shape shifting shamans
Of a lost proud tribe,
Actual alchemical creators
Not merely scribes.
We existed before words
And created the gods.

Every fool believes his words are wisdom… even me.

Tanzoism # 60

Daniel E. Tanzo

If You Really Want to know

Poetry is the gauntlet of the human existence,

from agony to ecstasy, mundane,

profane and sacred. From Christ on the cross

to Dionysian orgiastic debauchery

with nymphs who rend his flesh,

to the cry of a newborn babe,

reaching in and attaching itself to your soul

Poetry is life squared,

brought to existence,

through an oft times inadequate medium.

So we try to connect soul to soul,

with the ink from our veins.

Silk She Is

As we seek knowledge,

we discover the Universe is our classroom.
No wonder I had so many absences at school.

Tanzoism # 34

Daniel E. Tanzo

Go West Young Man nah

Where my soul abides
is where I rest.
I have littered the landscape
with bottles of my compulsions
changed to revulsions
taken too far and beyond.
Into each I pour what I shed and
no longer needed.
Glittering the byways of the Wild West.
They await the reclamation of one who would recycle
and redeem these bottles of ego intent.
So I shed the bottles of discontent
of that which no longer serves.
I must abide where my Soul resides
and hence my journey East.

Life is simple, but this simplicity is contingent upon trusting yourself, and trusting yourself can be confusing.

Tanzoism # 20

Daniel E. Tanzo

Trust yourself to walk your path,
the unmapped course,
its twists, turns,
dead ends and false starts,
that somehow lead you
to the panoramic view.
From atop the mountain,
and the depths of yourself

There's honesty and there's truth. The difference being:

In all honesty you may believe someone is your friend, but – the truth is, they are not

…Or that a happy meal is a good thing.

Tanzoism # 18

The greatest gift to be bestowed

is the teaching of the Sword.

That is to be present with others,

and thereby the Divine.

Upon its killing stroke

before bone and sinew

are torn asunder, and blood

is tendered.

It is at peace with itself,

its purpose known and guaranteed.

No past no future, just now.

Wisdom doesn't come from running after it;

it comes from standing still and letting the wind whisper to your soul.

Tanzoism # 45

Daniel E. Tanzo

Here lies…
and they always have
either to others
but most assuredly to
themselves.
Seen it often and
been at the effect of it
even more.
No more, no longer.
I failed and sent a
severance package.
With malice aforethought.
But it may have been the only way.
It seems my chute was built for one

The key to self-acceptance is – the ability to feel worthwhile, and lovable, despite your flaws.
The opposite is – refusal to believe you have any.

Tanzoism #17

Daniel E. Tanzo

What is it, the clinging grasp
to what you already abandoned?
That one foot still on the dock?
Is it you're just not sure of the boat
You're entering yet,
That's a coward's game that
drops you in the water

Silk She Is

Outdated and archaic beliefs have no place
in a modern logical thoughtful society.
We pretty much banned human sacrifice
so can we stop the witch hunts.

Tanzoism # 13

Daniel E. Tanzo

Do we truly hold dominion
to dominate and control
the misguided words from
an ancient text have wrought
hubris, and mournful soil.
Revise the book and return
the truth of our souls.
We are the stewards and tenders
of all we behold.
When Atlas shrugs, and shifts
the weight, the scales adjusted
shall find us worthy or wanting.

There is a profound difference between service and servitude. One lifts and exalts the spirit within from your actions; the other imposes the tyranny of another upon you in furtherance of a personal agenda.

Tanzoism # 31

Daniel E. Tanzo

Winter fears abated
spring upon the horizon
the reason for my season
fast approaching obscurity
lost amidst the flowers.
A warm and comforting space
now left for hopes of new embrace

Silk She Is

Shatter me

Burn me on the pyre

Unravel the fabric of my existence.

Fling the shards,

ashes and threads,

into the abyss.

Off to the far flung

corners of the Universe.

Just like God.

So I can learn

and return.

A candle in the dark.

Curses abated.

The abyss is where answers reside; release yourself to abide in Self.

Tanzoism # 4

Silk She Is

Be present

promise me no promises
for they are as ashes,
like the past and the future.
Be awareness, see tomorrow
be today, be that.
All that came, is done,
as is all that may be.
Be here now

Only by releasing can you attain what you seek. There comes a time when you begin finding perfection even in your less than perfect life.

Tanzoism # 16

Silk She Is

Where ya going?

Where have you been

Nowhere…

Welcome home then

For the truth is you never left.

Forgetting is not leaving.

The voice that whispered in the silence,

was you remembering

calling you back, to the palace you never left.

The mercurial events that comprise
the theater of our lives,
cannot define the sum of our souls.
It's the everyday mundane drudge,
that refines and polishes

Tanzoism # 23

Insulated Shell

Some people are content
spending their lives
in service of enterprises,
that contain no learning value
to themselves or others.
Set to circular patterns,
despite the cost.
They cannot bear
the heat of the forge.
Returning to the comfort of
same old same old.
Rain can either wash the skin
or rust the used-up armor.
That served not to protect the inside self,
but refuse the admittance of the outside.
A self-imposed shell,
that should be spelled 'cell'.
Take the journey not to foreign lands,
but the exotic one inside

There are so many people just living "on and off" this planet; so few actually living IN it.

Tanzoism # 52

Silk She Is

Run and race

chase chase chase

the elusive one thing

that's gonna make it better.

That if only "I" had this!

To find you could only see

one thing your whole life.

Is akin of a rock wishing to be the rain,

missing and dismissing every raindrop

that stopped to visit and lovingly

caressed its face.

Cynicism is a spiritual practice.

Tanzoism # 57

Silk She Is

Pursue Your Passion or STFU

Why waste a dream on mediocrity?
pursue your passion, whatever it may be
the purpose that makes you smile each day
Create your life to fill the cup of your soul.
If you bemoan your lack thereof
perhaps you haven't found your passion.
Though you scream to the Universe,
I want to sing, write, dance, teach, or heal.
If you sit around in misery
and 'why not me?'s,
perhaps your passion then is
just bitching.
Well then
be happy, you found it

Misery may love company,
but company rarely comes a-calling.

Tanzoism # 10

The Main Stream

The mainstream is now a cesspool.

Fed by nasty little estuaries of greed and disdain.

The Oracle no longer resides in Delphi

revered and honored.

She is now a pandering whore,

selling her wares, to those who defile

the tributaries from which we must drink.

Aiding and abetting while her coffers fill.

The Paradigm of the Universe is Paradox and Chaos.

Tanzoism # 63

Silk She Is

What does it say of a society of people, when doing
the accepted expected is the highest value,
and the second highest is
receiving the proper admiration of your peers,
for doing so?

What does it say?

Stagnation boredom and decay !
Doctor lawyer goverment drone,
false messiahs often cloned.

Praise us the pirates, poets, artists,
healers, teachers, singers, writers and
scoundrels.
For we not only live life, we adore it

If only common sense

spread as easily as the common cold.

Tanzoism # 1

Silk She Is

The House is bawdy,
only way to describe it.
Crammed with voices,
a feast of flesh
a song, a tempest.
Melodies entwine
sibilant thighs,
and breathful sighs

Daniel E. Tanzo

Your scent is on my ears
the color of your hair upon my hands
the flavor of your breath
remains on my tongue,
like nectar to the hummingbird.
Your fire ignites the water of
my blood, and every pore weeps
pleasure at the sight of you
striding towards me.

Silk She Is

You have taken residence
not like mice scurrying and scampering
with echoes of noise at night,
but like the honeysuckle vine
or blooming jasmine
… Calmly with casual elegance
wrapping and entwining
yourself with me.
Interlaced breaths
timed to rhythms of our blood
A convergence of paths
headed towards truths,
and nights, in bloom.

Daniel E. Tanzo

Sunset without you,

Memories of woman sitting

tendrils of smoke and sex hovering

stolen moments and promises

… Truth be told the Agony creates the Ecsatsy

Completeing the Bargain

Desires, dreams only thought,

and never dared spoken,

yet the score of the dance

Silk She Is

She knows of migratory hearts
and wandering eyes
the knowledge there in hers
unspoken
Too often the refrain
and pain of the moment.
Touches gone unnoticed
glances not returned.
Holding back the words
as little doors quietly close
the tick of locks for self preservation
protection and insulation.
In anticipation of a winter just begun.

There is no such thing as unwounded love;
It's the nature of love to be wounded
So growth may occur
So compassion, understanding,
and forgiveness strengthen in you.

Tanzoism # 44

Silk She Is

She speaks of my treacherous betrayal,
to others we both know.
Why is it those who do it so well,
seem to point it out so quickly?
It's because they are so intimate
with that with which they practice.
A master craftsman knows their craft.
Each stroke of brush, or curl of wood,
sliding off the awl.
I am not the engineer,
of this trainwreck.
I travel other paths, released
from rails of sychophants.

It's not how good the liar is, because few really are. It is, however, how much we want to believe the lie!

Tanzoism # 19

Gaia

Gaia weeps.

Her tears

falling birds

floating fish.

Crying out for retribution of her beloved's demise.

Kali her sister stirs and is awakened.

Let your thought, prayer or action today, be the one to change the world.

Tanzoism # 51

Silk She Is

At the feet of Kali
I bare my neck
in silent supplication
awaiting my sentence
Her sword descends
sealing my fate.
Sublime oblivion
inflation, deflation
the balloon of ego
rising and falling
the rollercoaster ride
of self.
the internal construct
of your own prison

For those who would journey inward to Self, being alone is not a curse, but the task.

Tanzoism # 46

Silk She Is

A voice carries the day
occurs in the night
A sleepy languorous huskied
honey glazed tenor.
Reaching past your lips
to my ear,
to travel through me
coursing as hounds after hares
through my veins.
A beckoning siren that whispers
'throw caution to the wind'
and speak forbidden words 'tween us.
I cannot not respond in my daydreams

Daniel E. Tanzo

Vision unfettered by presence
sees without sight.
What the stranger feels
by whisper of you passing.
My fingers journey the silhouette
of your feline grace,
panther's soul, gypsy's passion.
Journey's call aswered with
an affirmation to your purpose

Silk She Is

Trophies are for dusting, whether it be girlfriend, wife, or reminder of past accomplishments.

They speak to nothing more than a moment, and next week month or year.

Soon someone else has it on their mantle, and you're sitting alone looking at the place it once sat.

Live for this day's accomplishment, moment, or goal and stride purposely forward.

Laurel wreaths wither, dry and blow away; write new words for today.

Tanzoism # 22

Daniel E. Tanzo

Keep your bubble headed Barbies
fobs for your chains.
Give me Dorthy Parker and Anais Nin.
Unshackled women, who know of the flesh
and the pleasures within.
Cheroot smoking goddesses
who drink the witches' brew.
Warrior maidens, who know my cause.

Conforming is for the bland; the fence sitters of the world -- afraid to take a stand. It's for those afraid to laugh or cry, for those afraid to live or die. Moderation is lukewarm tea, the devil's own brew.

Tanzoism # 33

Daniel E. Tanzo

No Stick Figures

Bring me your curves
so I may surf the crest of your breasts
and ride voluptuous thighs
to the island's passage
where waves of delight
await us.
Hills and valleys reminders
of earth Mother
her burnished tawny skin
glazed with summer's sweat
allow my lips to rest
gently and gather sustenance
for my soul

Silk She Is

Instruction manuals

guides and pamphlets

how to books

and come hither looks.

you can read it but

you best learn how to breathe it

to truly know the woman

you must inhale her,

exhale yourself

Daniel E. Tanzo

Falling in Love with Truth is akin to being God's lover; the Ultimate Romance.

Tanzoism # 6

Silk She Is

Floating Away

Shall I tether you
a mooring
an anchor
in the sand
to ride the waves
but not float too distant?
If my fear requires that
my soul is not in play.
Our hearts are bonded,
corded, in so many stronger ways.
So sail as far needed,
each self the other's home.

Daniel E. Tanzo

I am the steady fall of rain.

The flame that burns.

The balm that soothes.

The pyre of ignited lovers.

Son of Mars,

Enamoured, lusting for battle.

Thor's hammer,

Child of Venus,

Lover of the Moon

Passion's Paramour

The loving arms,

Tender kiss.

Silk She Is

All the day we await our cue
the mystic's gift of gloaming
and all its many hues.
For that's when she sheds herself.
My lustful predator growl
is met with Panther's howl.
Mars collides with Venus,
and from there infernos form
which forged the Sun and life,
reflected in our eyes.
Where I cease she begins;
there is no separation.

Why is it that often a complex lie is easier to believe than a simple truth?

Tanzoism # 39

Silk She Is

When truth is forsaken
trust no longer binds,
A minor truth cannot obscure
this, return to your soul
where fear is just a word.
Then and only then
extend your hand to mine.
Across a sea or mountain,
extend your hand to mine,
waiting patiently.

The biggest lies are the ones we tell to ourselves.

Tanzoism # 38

Silk She Is

In search of that realm.

the sacred release from the mundane

where shadows gray,

obscure the day and reality is ours to command.

My lover fills my senses, like the breath of God.

Embattled lips bruised, sweat silked bodies,

curved like serpents joined.

Brazen mockery, of what's right or wrong.

Lifted eyes on ceilings seek and gather

me to her

The mind is like a dangerous neighborhood; you don't want to enter without serious weaponry. The heart is a better place to make decisions from.

Tanzoism # 36

Silk She Is

I get these bouts of madness
a dark and gruesome rage.
They stem from time spent closely
with a reaper of sanity.
The proximity just under the dermis
of icepicks, scratching, slicing through
the nerves, rubbed raw, by a simple breeze
or a mannequin standing there, looking at me.

Wearing a sarong is very conducive to calming one's nature.

Tanzoism # 11

Silk She Is

Clouds and Rain

My needs are upon me
a dormant flame rekindled.
I sense yours too,
At opposite ends of couch we reside
Legs bemoaning the touch
of your toes teasingly moving upward.
Toward my mouth, for the bawdy tongue
that awaits them.
Sending jolts of moisture higher
Opening the pasture to grazing.
My scalp pleads for your kneading fingers
my eyes your kneeling form, head turned aside
with wicked gracious smile,
an oasis awaits, provocation, invitation,
declaration of the blessings we are about to bestow.
Entwined hair with my clenched fist,
your back bowed and arched.
Teeth and breath,
upon your neck laid bare.
Matching bruises, and pulsing hearts
Echoing the arrival of the Clouds and Rain

The questing heart
in search of divine countenance
encounters itself.
In everything that is that,
or not that.
It cannot exclude this.

Tanzoism # 24

Silk She Is

Spring into my dreams

Alight with torches on a dark autumn eve
the fecund scent of fallen leaves our bedding
raise your fevered lips to my brow
annointing me with the sacrament of your heart.
A journey perilous, with traps of the past,
Dancing on the razor's edge

Daniel E. Tanzo

To me you're Cindy Lou Who
You entered quietly shyly
and spoke your truths.
Posing questions
… of this is that.
"Oh, you too have a cat."
I am me and who are you.
My heart got bigger
and so it grew ♥

Silk She Is

Release your guilt.

Guilt is a vainglorious game.

Not yours but mine,

the whip of power we flail ourselves with.

A testament of ego,

to the cudgel of our power.

That gaudy horsehair shirt we don,

wrapping our omnipotence in hubris

and humility, over our deity shadow.

mea culpa

et tu

Excessive guilt is a narcissistic enterprise.

Tanzoism # 62

Silk She Is

The yearning suppleness of desire
is not a stranger to my hands and lips
the cool fragrant lips above and fevered others
my nights sucumb to mistresses of the past
of wild tempetuous rides, and graceful acts
like acrobats, dancing.

Daniel E. Tanzo

This Needs No Explanation

What is this?
What?
What is this, this?
Oh? perhaps I'm obtuse
but I don't delve that deep.
Today is today and I revel in, this!
This, nourishes my soul,
whys and wherefores don't serve
one such as I.
A fool trusting a path
Am I shortsighted?
I hope so; the long sight is for
prophets and seers.
Peering into the expansive abyss:
I have always had this failing, if such it is so.
When I come to the cliff, where the dark beckons.
I LEAP and grow wings and soar where winds flow.
Buffeted by ill winds and tossed asunder,
rudderless never
for my heart is my compass

Silk She Is

The Why of It

I slip into your ease of being
it gathers and collects me.
If and perhaps I should,
remove my eyes.
And gift them to you for just a day.
Then maybe then you could come
to a place of seeing.
Perhaps all my senses for a day
and, a night?
To hear the voice,
that calls my name,
The hands that encompass your waist.
The heart that expands each day
at the thought of the soul I see.
Salt and earth of your skin
that my mouth is addicted to.
Perhaps then you would come to
knowing the why of it
This, this.

Daniel E. Tanzo

Two Boats Sail

Shown the depth of the mistaken belief
at the height of my despair.
One granted me sight to see the other
Shallow waters create a meager catch
Out of the bay my joy is heightened
a wave that lifts and allows me to soar down
the curved architechture riding with her
not swallowed submerged or subsumed.
Somehow we ride together on the crest
Seeing not depths but the summits that await

Silk She Is

You stride the day
and straddle me
challenging my beliefs
inquring as to this and that
laughingly, oh reallys
resound as chorus to our words
In silent witness I hold your grief
and appalud your strength.
Reflections cast upon the same mirror

Daniel E. Tanzo

C'mere, I'll help you find the way
back to that place
where everything is brighter
tastes better
and when you stroll
down the street
men will sigh
and know
there goes a woman well tended
to the depths of herself
and know they are better for it
your fleeting passage

Silk She Is

I take a step upward

into the depth of you.

Treading with feline grace,

prowling for your core.

Paying homage to the Guardian at the gate.

The protective belt and Divine testament

to source and devotion

Arrival heralded with pre-emptory caution,

I meet the Innocent with mine.

A shy agreement sealed with smiles

Daniel E. Tanzo

Release your fear like
a flock of white doves
to soar apart of you.
Let it find its roost elsewhere,
it has no place here among
… you and I.
Where we reside
cannot be entered
with such a burden.
Fear is an anchor to the soul.
Let it fly and be with timid ones.
Cross the threshold
to answers seeking questions.
And songs seeking words

Silk She Is

In the darkness
today, 'tis yours I feel
that deep sadness
held in abeyance by the
flippant remark and smile
it's the smile that
speaks the gray musty
pain, dulled but ever clear.
In the corner of the lips,
there deep in shadows of your eyes
past the facade into the
abyss
where you scream
silently your fear,
that you may be worshipped
but not loved.
Viewed but not seen

Fear is often more infectious than faith or love. It's why politicians and ministers use it

Tanzoism # 59

Silk She Is

A veil descends

Soul's search ascends,

To rise above obscurity,

a mortal's fears

of loss and gain.

A strong belief,

like Autumn leaf.

Shall rise again come Spring

Daniel E. Tanzo

An Uncharted Isle

I have come to this island
as penitent and explorer
my soul weary from years
of ocean's travels.
Many ports of call, exotic lands,
and desert dunes.
I now rest easy,
no longer besotted
with youthful haste.
I now know the way to range
and map an island.
Tenderly travel its coast,
committing to memory
its contours, coves and shoals.
Then the streams and rivers
and all the tributaries.
Only then do I travel to the dark torrid rain forest
the heart and core of you.
For you are this Island.
Seemingly quiet
with Volcanic core

Silk She Is

"I love you," she whispered that night

I had her repeat it.

Another whisper entered the room,

"Hold on, this is going to hurt,

more than anything has before."

Both voices were telling the Truth

One still is.

Daniel E. Tanzo

The Contract

With enduring sigh
words returned,
to what are you committed?
His reply, to life and laughter
and one more thing
And what is that, she asked?
He smiles and quietly speaks,
That which you see in the mirror each day
To whom do I speak and share,
and lay beside?
After 40 years the answer is always
the same.
I do

Silk She Is

Blessed escape

You must flay me,
wear my skin,
upon your own.
Show me how to touch you
be my guide through terra firma
of rounded mounds and
glorious clefts, creases
and chasms of your
sacred grounds
be my lips, eyes and hands

Learn to love your burdens; they are also your blessings

Tanzoism # 48

Silk She Is

To live from get to
rather than have to,
an adjustment seemingly
absurdly simple.
Duty becomes desire,
To share one's day with
the one who loves you.
Not a burden but a blessing.
These foggy moments,
of memory, are hers not mine.
I remember, that's my get to.
I'm here because I want to.
Never have to.

Daniel E. Tanzo

Grizzlies make poor care givers,
lumbering grumbling
cantankerous rancorous
blundering bumbling
puzzled befuddled
wondering, where did she go?

(written the first week after mom's second stroke, adjusting finally)

Developing compassion for others creates a road back from self-loathing.

Tanzoism # 2

Daniel E. Tanzo

Beauty is a living thing
inside you,
it's in your laughter and your toes
The trailing tresses, and laughing eyes.
I know you from
inside the song of you,
the beat of your breath
upon my ear.
Foolish others, blinded by self,
now confined upon shelves.
Bound by the ignorance of their actions
Beauty is in the eye of the beholder.
I am beholding to you

The Ultimate Beauty of Truth,

is that Belief or Faith play no part in its occurrence.

Rest in Truth and Abide in Beauty

Tanzoism # 7

Daniel E. Tanzo

Seeded Souls

Beauty that sows seeds,
in the soul like flowers,
in the eye of the beholder, remains.
beauty may perish, and beholder die,
The soul in which the flower grows,
Survives

I'm so damned enlightened, I have transcended ego.
Thus spoke -EGO

Tanzoism # 25

Daniel E. Tanzo

The tallest tree,
the most vibrant flower,
are always noticed,
the brash and bold are envied.

By illuminating self, shadows emerge

to grapple with their lack and bring you into

the fold of drab

Tanzoism # 29

Life is to Love

By Grace through Action
Know your Soul
by your Actions
be Truly kind to People.

Daniel love nothing
or love all.
Regardless love
for if it's love,
it creates no pain

Love is the dormant seed
buried beneath a glacier.
patiently awaiting the
sunlight's first kiss.
or not

Dealing with your Shadow is akin to dealing with a profligate liar. You just have to keep poking holes in the story until the holes eventually are plugged with Light

Tanzoism # 61

Daniel E. Tanzo

Come dance with the shadow in
that place of darkened pastures,
At cliff's edge, teetering at
Salvation's cost,
There is no safety from your self.
Learn and tell no lies,
to lie is to deny and be incomplete.
To acknowledge is not to act the deed.
Rather more a nod to self, replete

Come dance with me
you know you want to, throw caution to the wind
a heady night engulfed in flaunting societies modality
run and embrace the wicked girl inside you
the one that knows the truth of
that which is denied is sweeter all the more
The moon is silent; it keeps all secrets
whisper to her the vaulted thoughts
that wander across your mind, safely.
There is no safety from your self

Silk She Is

Come dance with me by the pale moonlight

> throwing caution to the wind
> hands, my hands
> scarred dark and battered
> like sandpaper on velvet
> … hands, your hands
> tracing the ink in my soul
> where your name was written
> inscribed there at my birth
> waiting only for your descent

Come dance

> in the flickering shadows
> alive, alive
> on the canvas of the moon
> cast off the everyday
> Let me hear your cry
> Alive, alive
> From across the mountain
> I'll answer your call
> with the howl of knowledge
> of she released from
> the bondage of
> sun.

Daniel E. Tanzo

My favorite sound is woman's tone.

It reaches to me from the clatter
of high heeled shoes.
The sussing sound of skirts,
and flash of crystal laughter.
Eyes speaking promises
Flippant remarks of tousled hair
Ruby lips parted releasing sighs
When I have bared her to the bone.
My favorite sound is woman's tone.

Silk She Is

The tone of your laughter
is woman's tone,
that particularly pleasant sound
that reaches down through me.
Crystallized amber and honey,
past my mouth from yours
like a kiss of lovers,
the taste of each other
melded in us.
A symphony of delight
written just for me.
How is this accomplished?

Daniel E. Tanzo

Is love the cure

or the disease?

that crawls inside me and

brings us to our knees.

My thoughts consumed

of primal rides

galloping to a crest.

Dropping down from your breast

whispering breath upon a rose

to drink and quench

from flowing font.

Throat exposed and gaze

aloft.

quietly whispered

again oh yes again

Silk She Is

Shall we Dance
Across a continent divide
tentative glances
… collide

Where the wall meets
the ceiling is where I live
that peculiar perch.
Where your face resides
each night
a wraith that accompanies me
A gypsy dancing in my dreams

Daniel E. Tanzo

Wicked Girl

Bitter struggle

Lying fallen

Stones cold

'neath anguished flesh

Arms aloft

Wrists crossed

Held fast

Ragged breath

Eyes averted

Neck exposed

Desperate Writhing

Slowly… smiling

Oh.

Wicked.

Wicked girl

beneath me

shackled

heaving heart

waiting for the truth.

who truly?

is captive

to the moment

Silk She Is

She arrived on the wings of a crow

Brazen and raucous,
demanding her due
Henna'd tresses flung in defiance
Eye to eye bold warriors challenge
to be truly met and honored
in the halls of Valhalla
To rock in his arms
the child inside
to feel the tears
of all the years
that passed without
a glance
he held and cooed
to both he and you
the words oft desired
the touch we both craved
someone please love me
someone please see
how beautiful I am
be glad that I be

Daniel E. Tanzo

The kind of friend you are

without knowing of my thirst

you quenched it

with the spark of your eyes

truth of your words

love of your soul

you pumped the bellows and rekindled

the fire of the forge

tempering the

the steel of the man

a new sword

for battle of self

Silk She Is

Yours is the face I knew before
being born
The voice that arrives on slivers
of the silent moon
The voice of patience and longing
whispers of promise
that voids my words, deeds and thoughts
don't speak

What we shared is,
just as true now as then,
so we cope and care
and revel in what was
with winsome smiles
each on speed dial
well placed bets
no regrets

Daniel E. Tanzo

Can she ever be all mine?

Her mouth like wine and valentine

Voice like string of pearls

still dripping with juice of oyster

She loves me all she can,

… can she ever be all mine?

Can I or any other know her;

to the part of herself

she may not heed or see

She loves me all she can

Silk She Is

Bribery

Those twin ten digit foundations
that support those pillars.
So shapely, as if turned
by a master cratsman
on his lathe.
Sentinels which my
encroaching hands must lull
into a somnambulant conspiracy.
Rhythmically, hypnotically, inducing
Acquiescence, and a parting of thighs.
With grace and stealth of cat burglar
I tease n turn the tumblers quietly, deftly
and upon hearing your sigh,
knowing the contents of the vault
a predator's guttaral growl is released.
Caution is no longer heeded,
your alliance is broken
new treaties must be drawn

If you want to drive the car you better warm the engine

Tantric Tanzoism # 1

Silk She Is

Pearlescent comingled juices on
sheets tangled with sweat laden loins
meshing and threshing
mournful breaths and soulful sighs
traces of kisses purple n dark
...territorial claims, proclaiming
an unabashed mastering
slaves to passions of seasons
when the sanguinary frenzy
abandons

And twixt tangled sheets
where parted thighs are quenched,
your cries feed my frenzy.

Daniel E. Tanzo

A Most Dangerous Woman

You fill my days

you are never not with me,

Upon awakening, my eyes rest

upon your hair, there beside me.

Then thoughts of the meal,

I shall make of you,

to break my fast.

A languid turning of myself

to stretch the length of you.

I run my finger over the rounded mound

of your flaring hip, hearing your yelp

when I make my first nibbling venture

along your spine at the cleft of your ass.

I cannot not roll you, to garner my sustenance

at the banquet displayed so flagrantly before me.

With a, "Good morning, Mr. Tanzo. Please proceed."

I am given leave to consume her.

Fire flamed eyes meet mine,

in the darkened gloom

of curtained room, a whisper comes,

"I'm hungry, too"

A tousled tussling shift occurs,

my turn to moan,

as she pays homage to

the seed bearer

A Most Dangerous Woman indeed

Silk She Is

With finger of magician
or an old card shark,
she filched the last chocolate
from the box.
With a frown I protested.
(I dearly love truffles)
Taunting eyes and sinister lips
the morsel at her mouth,
she says, you want it,
come get it.
I reach, it disappears
Uh-uh, no hands, she admonishes.
We tussle and wrestle for the prize.
Our weapons of choice jousting
suddenly becoming allies.
creating peaceful coexistence

Daniel E. Tanzo

An Extraordinary Approach

Every day I must begin anew
for she always is, reborn.
As during night she fled and traveled
countless worlds and under lands
Obscure jungles and desert 'scapes,
prowling as panther or soaring as
a dusky-hued raven bearing
a message to herself.
Visiting me in her heart,
where I abide patiently
awaiting the call of dawn.
To believe in my hubris
I know this creature and
all her ways is folly.
The world has turned
traveled great distances
while appearing to stand still.

Silk She Is

How can I believe it is she from yesterday,
or I am myself as far as that goes?
So I approach the ordinary day
with extraordinary mission.
to once again seduce her,
by keeping myself quiet.
Each kiss a first upon her throat
lips and eyes, a brand new
breast awakens to my teasing fingers
and petals enflamed by touch.
Her sighs a siren's song calling
beguiling revealing anew

We Have Yet to Meet, but Each Night we Speak

I delight in your presence,

I yearn to please you in the quiet secret alcove,

where passion for my touch resides in you.

The face reserved for public consumption slips,

and the gypsy is revealed.

My lover, who craves the touch of my hands,

lips and loins.

Whom I bring pleasure to in a moist

and convulsive manner.

She dreams of erotic entanglements,

of our well matched weaponry,

jousting 'till reposed and

panting for breath.

Sand

I am the sands of the beach,
patiently waiting for you, the wave,
to caress me with your visits.
Throughout the day.
I am the wind and you the leaves in the tree
who whisper and bring memories of the sun's warmth
to travel the length of you into your roots.
I am the roots, and you the underground spring
from which I am nourished.
You are the spring that feeds the oceans
and I, the sands on the beach,
await patiently
for your caress.

Daniel E. Tanzo

G'nite Mr. Tanzo

Is how each night ends
The formality much
more intimate somehow.
Out of the myriad of possibilities
And centuries past, flowing with
the infinte permutations
leading to our singular lives.
Now adding the the number
of those occupying the same time.
Chance is how we met,
ok if you say so.
Funny but we don't somehow.

Silk She Is

The other drum bangs slowly or quickly,
it matters not, for others can't hear it,
but for those that can and do
Here's to us:
the pirates, poets, writers,
singers, musicians,
teachers and healers,
who not only live life,
but Adore IT

Tanzoism # 27

Godspeed, Dan.
Until we meet again.

In Love and Light,
The Wolf Pack

Silk She Is
Poetry by Daniel E. Tanzo
Compiled and edited by Mandy White
Cover design by Mandy White
Published by WPaD Publications

Daniel E. Tanzo

Made in the USA
San Bernardino, CA
06 April 2014

ST. MARY'S COLLEGE OF MARYLAND
ST. MARY'S CITY, MARYLAND

THE BLIND MUSICIAN.

THE BLIND MUSICIAN.

(FROM THE RUSSIAN OF KOROLENKO.)

BY

SERGIUS STEPNIAK,
AUTHOR OF "RUSSIA UNDER THE TZARS," &c.,

AND

WILLIAM WESTALL,
AUTHOR OF "THE OLD FACTORY," "NIGEL FORTESCUE," &c.

GREENWOOD PRESS, PUBLISHERS
WESTPORT, CONNECTICUT

Originally published in 1890
by Ward and Downey, London

First Greenwood Reprinting 1970

Library of Congress Catalogue Card Number 69-13961

SBN 8371-4093-5

Printed in the United States of America

INTRODUCTION.

THE young Russian author, whose work we have the honour of introducing to English readers, is not altogether a stranger to those who are interested in Russian fiction. In the periodical reviews of current Russian literature published in the *Athenæum*, the name of Vladimir Korolenko almost always holds a conspicuous place. Mr. C. E. Turner, English lecturer in the University of St. Petersbourg, in his excellent book upon modern Russian novelists (a reprint of his six lectures in the London Institute), devotes a whole chapter to Korolenko, whom he rightly considers as the most gifted and popular among our living authors, Tolstoi, of course, excepted.

The brief literary career of Korolenko has been indeed a series of brilliant successes. His first sketches were published about eight years ago, soon after his return from oriental Siberia, where he had spent a few years as a political exile. The best of these sketches were inspired by the country where he was an involuntary guest. They reveal a wonderful gift of artistic reproduction of what is called local colouring, both in nature and in people's lives. As to the individual characters, they are drawn cleverly and correctly, but, with few exceptions, they are rather sketchy, presenting only the outlines of living persons.

Later on the author showed a keen psychological insight, sometimes even slipping into excess. But it seems as though in these early days his soul was so deeply stirred by the wonders of the outward world as to leave little room for the observation of individuals. But when some type of humankind strongly attracted his attention by its exceptional power or weakness, as, for example, the "Ubivez" in a story of the same name, and Makar in "Makar's Dream," he showed that he can achieve much even in the most difficult domain of character drawing.

"The Blind Musician," which appeared in 1885, shows Korolenko's talent in quite a new light. It is above all a psychological story, the interest being focussed upon one individual, the blind boy, who afterwards becomes a musician.

It was a bold venture on the author's part to undertake to render comprehensible an inward life so exceptional and so different from our own. But all those who read this touching story will agree that he has succeeded marvellously. We can not say by what wonder of intuition he came to know all he tells us about the inward life of this extraordinary boy. But we feel that all he says is true, which is the great triumph of art.

At times the young author seems to be himself carried away by the superabundance of his creative power, and enters into minute psychological details which would do honour to a scientific treatise, but are out of place in a work of art.

We took the liberty of omitting these superfluous subtleties. Our excuse for thus interfering with so exquisite a work is that the English, who are very particular in these matters—and rightly so—could not stand them at all. So that our alternative was either to let this gem of modern Russian fiction remain unknown, or to take upon ourselves to omit what retards the action as well as the development of character and weakens instead of strengthening the general impression. Similar considerations induced us to omit with regret several allusions to the early history of the Ukrainian Cossaks, which means so much for a fellow countryman of the author, but would be quite incomprehensible to the English—unless we disfigured the book with numerous foot-notes.

INTRODUCTION. vii

We had also to modify the passage (chap. xvii.) referring to the *colour* of music, which cannot be rendered in any foreign language, because there is no equivalent to the Russian words "red" or "crimson" chimes, upon which these ingenious inferences are based,—a fact which proves that they are chance metaphors and not a revelation of any secret of our common nature.

The difficulty of both the discovery and rendering of some psychological trait has as little to do with the artistic value of a work of fiction as the difficulty of performance with the merits of a musical composition. The charm and artistic value of "The Blind Musician" does not lie there. It depends upon the eternally human element which the author has so admirably developed upon his exceptional background. The scene of the first meeting of the two children, Petrik and Velia, upon the hill —so simple and yet so full of truth and poetry—is artistically superior to all the subtle passages concerning the blind boy's spiritual growth—except perhaps the scene of the revelation of his musical genius whilst listening to the stable-boy's pipe. And we think that the character which lifts this story above the rank of a "study," as the author has modestly called it, is not that of the elaborated Petrik, but of the simple Evelina, in whom Korolenko has created a new and fresh type of Slavonic women, which does not pall even by the side of Turgueneff's heroines.

Velia is a girl of homely virtues, unable by nature to be fixed with any broad, social, or political idea. The scenes of her temptations chap. xiii.) show precisely this.

The two young men—the Stavruchenkos—who come to pay a visit to Petrik's family and try to make her swerve from the path she has traced for herself, are revolutionists--"Nihilists," to use the popular term—who are on the point of starting upon revolutionary propaganda among the peasants. What they propose to her is to join hands with them in the common work for the liberation of their country. This is not put quite clearly in the story. Russian authors are not allowed to speak plainly of such matters, and we could not do more in the text than give the plain meaning to some purposely vague expressions of the original. But for the Russians, who understand the language of allusions, there can be no doubt as to the significance of these scenes. For one moment Velia seems aroused, but that moment passes; she is not born for political heroism, but for the modest work of devotions and sacrifice in home life. It is a striking testimony to Korolenko's artistic gift, that in a time when all are captivated with the opposite type of women, he was able to feel the beauty of this one and reproduce it with such delicacy of touch and depth of conception. In him we have a born artist, a man whose impressions of life are too keen and vivid to allow him to see it distorted by any preconceived political or philosophical theory. He is both the most objective and thoroughly sane of our young writers, which is not the least pledge of his future achievements.

"The Blind Musician" is not the best we can expect from Korolenko. Last year he published in a Russian magazine two short fragments entitled, "In Two Moods." By the richness and variety of colour, the comprehensiveness of the subject and the mastery of the workmanship, these short disconnected pieces stand as much above "The Blind Musician" as the latter is above his early sketches. We doubt not that in Korolenko we have a writer who will become one of the glories of Russia, and who will be known and appreciated not in Russia alone. But there is a peculiar charm in watching a young talent whilst in the process of its growth, and it is in the belief that this feeling may be shared by the many lovers of Russian fiction in this country that we publish this story.

S. STEPNIAK.

THE BLIND MUSICIAN.

CHAPTER I.

The child was born at midnight in the house of his father, a rich Ruthenian noble.

The young mother lay half unconscious, with closed eyes, but when the babe's first plaintive cry reached her ear she tossed restlessly on the pillow, her lips moved, and over the pale delicate face, with its refined features, flitted an expression of impatient suffering, like that of a child troubled with an unwonted sorrow. The nurse, bending her head to the lady's lips, heard faintly whispered these words:

"Why—why is he——?"

The nurse, failing to understand the question,

was about to turn away, when the babe cried again; and again a look of keenest anguish passed over the mother's face, and a tear-drop welled from her still closed eyes.

"Why—why is he——?" she repeated in a scarcely audible whisper.

"Oh! You mean why is he crying? Babies always cry. There is nothing to be uneasy about. The doctors say it does them good."

But the mother refused to be comforted. At every fresh cry of her child she visibly shuddered and went on repeating:—

"Why—why does he cry so—so pitifully?"

The nurse, seeing nothing unusual in the crying of a young child, thought that her mistress must be slightly delirious, and leaving the bedside gave all her attention to the little stranger.

Presently the lady ceased her murmurings. But now and then, as if some hidden sorrow, or dark foreboding too deep for words, were gnawing at her heart, tears would filter through her long dark eyelashes and trickle slowly down her colourless cheeks.

Was she, as the nurse supposed, delirious, or did her mother's heart tell her that her little one had come into the world bearing a cross—that he was the victim of a terrible calamity, a calamity which would overshadow his life from the cradle to the grave.

The child was born blind, yet for a while nobody —with the possible exception of the mother—suspected the truth.

The boy seemed to look before him with that vague and stolid gaze which is common to all nurselings up to a certain age.

Day followed day, and the life of the new-born man could be reckoned by weeks. Yet though his eyes became clearer and the pupils could be distinctly traced, there was a look—an indefinable something—which differentiated him from other young children. He never turned his head to follow the ray of light that streamed into the room, together with the joyous warbling of birds and the rustling of the young birch trees, which waved their leafy boughs before the window.

The mother, who had by this time regained her strength, observed with deepening alarm the portentous strangeness of her boy's face. It was always so immutably and unchildishly grave. She fluttered about him like a frightened bird, asking all and sundry who came into the nursery the same question.

"Do you know? Oh, tell me, why is he like that? So strange!"

"Like what?" was the invariable answer. "I see no strangeness in him. He is just like other babies."

"But don't you see how strangely he feels for everything with his little hands?"

"The child cannot, as yet, co-ordinate the movements of his hands with his optical impression," explained the surgeon, to whom, for the twentieth time, she had put the same question.

"But why are his eyes always fixed? as if—my God! he is—he is blind!"

After this terrible suspicion had taken root in the mother's mind she refused to be comforted.

The surgeon, taking the child into his arms, turned it rapidly to the light, and then looked intently into its eyes.

For a moment he seemed doubtful, and then, muttering some meaningless excuse, left the house. The next day he came again, bringing with him his ophthalmoscope. Taking a lighted candle, he moved it to and fro before the boy's eyes; next, using the ophthalmoscope, he looked several times into the child's eyes. The more he looked the graver became his face.

"Madam," he said, turning to the mother, and speaking in a voice of deep compassion, "madam, you were unfortunately not mistaken. Your son is blind, and I fear—I am sorry to say—that I do not think there is the slightest possibility of a cure."

The mother listened with calm sadness.

"I knew it—knew it long ago," she said in a low voice.

CHAPTER II.

IN addition to the young mother and the child, the family consisted merely of the father and Uncle Maxim, as everybody in the neighbourhood called Lady Popelsky's only brother.

The father was a genial good-natured man, kind to his labourers and tenants, but so given to building and rebuilding that he had little leisure for aught else. Indeed, save at meal times and bed time, he was seldom in the house. On these occasions, however, he never failed to inquire with affectionate solicitude after his wife's health, and then, unless he had some new thing to tell about his building enterprises, he would relapse into his habitual silence.

It need hardly be said that this guileless and

taciturn country gentleman had little influence on the inner life of his son or the development of his character.

Uncle Maxim was a man of another stamp. Ten years before his nephew's birth he had been noted, not only in all the country side but also in Kieff, for his quarrelsome, turbulent disposition, and everybody was afraid of him. He had fought several duels, and was so good a shot and skilful fencer withal, that his adversaries always came off second best. The gentry of the district could not understand how the Lady Popelsky (born Tazenko) came to have so terrible a brother. Although his fellow nobles did their best not to provoke their dangerous neighbour to wrath he almost invariably met their very courteous advances with studied insolence. On the other hand, Uncle Maxim allowed the common folk to take liberties with him which any other gentleman of his quality would have resented with blows. In the end, to the great joy of all respectable people, he conceived a violent hatred for the Austrians and went to Italy, where he got his fill of fighting under the banner of Garibaldi, a man as wild and turbulent as himself, who, as the nobles of the neighbourhood told each other, had struck up a friendship with the devil, and set the Holy Father himself at defiance, thereby, as they firmly believed, losing his heretical soul for ever. But though he may have lost others gained. Social gatherings became as peaceful as of yore; mothers no longer feared for their sons, sisters for their brothers.

For a long time nothing was heard of Maxim, but one fine day the *Little Courier*, a local print, which was supposed to keep the gentry of the province informed as to the affairs of the outer world, told its readers that in an encounter with the Austrians Tazenko's horse had been shot and himself cut to pieces.

"A bad end for a gentleman of his condition," observed his former neighbours to each other, and they piously ascribed Maxim's death, of which they made no doubt, to the special interposition of St. Peter in favour of his successor.

But they were wrong. Maxim was not dead. The Austrian swords had failed to drive his obstinate soul out of his sturdy body. He was rescued by his cut-throat Garibaldian comrades, carried to a place of safety, and cured, as far as possible, of his wounds.

A few years later Maxim appeared unexpectedly at his sister's house, of which he became thenceforth a permanent inmate. But his fighting days were over. He had lost his right leg, and his left hand was so mutilated as to be practically useless. Also, he had become much more serious and sedate; yet now and then, when anything provoked him, his tongue would give blows as sharp and well aimed as those which he had once dealt with his redoubtable sword. He went no more to fairs and social gatherings, paid no visits and passed most of his time reading in the library. As to the nature of his studies, nothing was known; rumour, however, had it that they were decidedly heretical, if not positively godless. It was likewise rumoured that he wrote for publication; but as none of his productions appeared in the *Little Courier* this story lacked confirmation and was only believed by a credulous few.

At the time of his nephew's birth Maxim was a middle-aged gentleman, with grizzly hair, and his outward seeming was not of a sort to inspire either admiration or respect at first sight. His crutches had forced up his shoulders nearly to a level with his ears, thereby giving his still stalwart though mutilated body the semblance of a square. His swarthy face, seamed with an ugly scar, his sternly knitted brows, the clatter of his crutches as he stumped about in a cloud of smoke from the short pipe which was ever in his mouth; all this, besides marking the old soldier as a being apart, repelled casual acquaintances and half frightened to death children who saw him for the first time. Only his kinsfolk and intimates knew that in the maimed body beat a warm heart, and that in the square head, covered with short dark bristles, an active brain was always at work.

At first Uncle Maxim gave little heed to the blind boy. What mattered it whether there was a human being more or less in the world? But gradually, and almost unconsciously, he became interested in the poor little man. There was a similarity in their conditions, both being equally unfitted for the battle of life, which kindled his sympathy and touched his heart.

"Humph," he growled one day, casting a side glance at his nephew, "this boy is as helpless as I am. Put together we might make one passable man."

Yes, the boy was hopelessly blind. Not all the skill of the faculty, not all the prayers of the Church might give to those vacant yet beautiful eyes the power of sight.

CHAPTER III.

COULD it be that, wittingly or unwittingly, aught had been done, by the boy's parents or others, to bring about this dire misfortune? Impossible! Even the immediate cause of the blindness could not be ascertained; it lay hidden deep in the obscure and complicated operations of nature. Yet Lady Popelsky never looked at her babe that the question did not mingle with her thoughts and trouble her peace. Reason and fact to the contrary notwithstanding, there lurked in her heart a half-belief that those who were responsible for her boy's being were in some mysterious way answerable for his affliction. This thought and the mother's love for her sightless child made him the chief interest of her life and the unconscious despot of the family—a despot whose very whims had to be respected, and whose wishes were no sooner known than they were implicitly obeyed.

What in these circumstances would have become

of the blind boy—all the household conspiring to ruin his character beyond redemption—what would have become of him had the Austrian swords which drunk Uncle Maxim's blood taken also his life, it is hard to say. It almost seemed as if he had been saved from his enemies for the very purpose of rescuing this young life from the kindness of his kin.

The advent and growth of the blind boy gave a special turn to the maimed warrior's meditations. For hours together he would sit in a nimbus of tobacco-smoke, thinking and observing, and the longer he observed the oftener he knitted his brows, the more fiercely he puffed at his pipe and the denser grew the smoke-cloud.

At last he resolved to interfere.

"That boy," he said, speaking from the cloud, "that boy is more unfortunate even than I am. It would have been better had he never been born."

His sister bowed her head, and her eyes filled with tears.

"Max, it is cruel—cruel to remind me of it to no purpose," she answered reproachfully.

"I say nothing but the truth, as you well know. Though I have lost a leg and most of my fingers, I have eyes. The boy has no eyes, and in the time to come he will have neither legs nor arms, nor any mind worth speaking of."

"Why, what—what mean you, Maxim?"

"Listen, Anna!" returned her brother, relaxing his rugged brows and speaking in a more kindly tone. "I would not for the world say cruel things to no purpose. I have a purpose. The boy is of a nervous, highly-strung temperament. His other senses may probably be so developed as to make up in a measure for the sense which he lacks; but to this end he needs exercise, and exercise comes only from necessity. Your fond solicitude, by anticipating all his wants and depriving him of all need of exertion, is destroying in him the germs of a fuller life in the future."

Anna Mikailovna, Lady Popelsky, was a woman of sense, and, seeing that her brother was right, she took the hint, and thenceforth refrained from rushing headlong to the child at his first cry. Left to himself, the blind boy crept freely and frequently all over the house, feeling with rapid and agile fingers everything that came in his way or could be reached with his hands.

Very soon he could recognize his mother by her footsteps, by the rustling of her gown, and by other signs incomprehensible to the full-sighted. He would find her even in a room about which guests were ever on the move. If she took him unexpectedly in her arms he would instantly lisp her name. Did any other body take him, he would pass his fingers deftly over his captor's face, and in this way soon learnt to distinguish his father, his uncle and his nurse. But when he found himself in the arms of a stranger, the movements of the little hands were slower, the boy moved his fingers over the unknown face more carefully, and his own assumed a look of deepest attention. He was observing through his hands. He was of an intelligent lively nature, and quick of comprehension. Yet as time went on his blindness began to affect both his character and his temper. The vivacity of his movements gradually diminished. He would spend hours in some out-of-the-way corner, sitting quite still, his face expressionless, and listening intently. When the house was hushed and there were no outward sounds to disturb his attention he seemed to be deep in thought, and there gradually settled on his speaking countenance, with its sightless eyes, a look of grave, unchildlike perplexity.

Uncle Maxim had correctly diagnosed his nephew's character. The boy's nervous, highly-strung temperament was beginning to manifest itself, striving to reach the fulness of its impressions through the senses of hearing and touch. The subtlety of his touch was extraordinary. It almost seemed as if he could distinguish with his fingers one colour from another. Handling a piece of bright coloured cloth gave him more pleasure than handling one that was dark or dull.

But his acutest sense, the sense of hearing, developed the most rapidly, and gave him the greatest satisfaction. He learned to distinguish one room from another by their characteristic sounds. He could tell by the peculiar crackling of his uncle's chair when he sat down, knew by the dry rustling of the thread when his mother was sewing, and recognized his father by the ticking of his watch.

When groping his way along the walls the blind boy would stop suddenly short, listen to some light sound inaudible to everybody else, and then, raising his hand, make a futile attempt to catch a fly, whose fairylike footsteps he had faintly heard. He could not account for the creature's disappearance; but the next moment he would be all eagerness, listening intently to the beating of its tiny wings, and turning his eyes to the point whither it was wending.

The moving, resounding, glaring external world penetrated into the blind boy's brain mostly in the form of sounds, wherewith he had to build up his conceptions of the life which he could never see. Intent listening became the fixed expression of his face. He went about with knitted brows and bent head, the beautiful, albeit motionless eyes imparting to his features a look which, though somewhat stern and sombre, was nevertheless unspeakably touching and pathetic.

CHAPTER IV.

Time went on.

The second winter of the blind boy's life drew to a close. The snow fled from the fields, and the streamlets, glad harbingers of spring, murmured sweet music in their pebbly beds.

Having been kept indoors during the long winter, Petrik had suffered both in health and spirits; but when the days lengthened, and the double sashes were removed from the windows, and the happy springtide came up from the south, his spirits rose and his health improved. The sun looked brightly into the child's playroom, flooding it with light. Showers of diamonds fell softly from the tree-tops and sank into the ground; the meadows, freed from their wintery winding sheets, put on their livery of spring, and myriads of tiny creatures, wakening up from their long sleep, rejoiced in the renewed activity of their mother earth.

For the blind boy spring-time was an irruption of hurrying sounds. He heard the sonorous gurgling of the rivulets as they rushed in tempestuous rout through their deep channels, freshly cut in the soft moist mould. The branches of the beech trees whispered to the windows, and beat against the panes with light rhythmical touches. The icicles, as they fell from the eaves and clashed merrily on the ground, made a hundred different tunes. All these sounds flowed into the room, now like volleys of many-coloured pebbles, now like a rapid and fitful roll of distant thunder. Sometimes the cry of a flock of cranes, as they sailed through the sky, would break sharply above the incessant din, and then die out, as if melting slowly into the air.

To this reawakening of nature Petrik's face responded with a look of pained perplexity. He knitted his brows, stretched his neck, listening intently, and then, as if half frightened by the incomprehensible Babel of sounds, put out his hands towards his mother, and clung to her, trembling.

"What can be the matter with the child?" wondered Lady Popelsky.

"Just what I have been asking myself," said Uncle Maxim, who had been carefully watching his nephew through a cloud of tobacco-smoke. "Just what I have been asking myself. Why should the poor little man be so agitated?"

"There is something he does not understand," said Lady Popelsky as Petrik turned his wistful face to hers.

She had guessed aright. There was something the child did not understand. The old sounds to which he was accustomed were gone, and new sounds, which he could not make out, had taken their place.

But soon the last vestiges of winter had vanished, spring took full possession of the earth, and under the warm solar rays the revival of nature went on with ever-increasing rapidity, like the speed of a newly-started train. The fields were glorious in their daisy-pied mantles of verdure; the birds were singing, the sweet smell of fresh birch buds filled the air; and one fine day the boy was taken out for a walk, his mother leading him by the hand, Uncle Maxim crutching by his side. Their objective point was a little hillock near the river, which the sun and wind had thoroughly dried. It was covered with thick grass and commanded an extensive view.

Petrik clung nervously to his mother, her forefinger tightly clasped in his tiny hand. But the excitement of the moment and the beauty of the prospect rendered her temporarily oblivious to this sign of the child's agitation. Had she glanced at him she would have seen that he was almost beside himself. His sightless, wide-open eyes were turned towards the sun in mute wonder, and through his parted lips he breathed the fresh air in gulps, like an exhausted runner. His face bespoke rapt delight, then bewilderment, and, finally, something akin to fear.

On reaching the hill-top all three sat down on the turf. When Lady Popelsky lifted the boy up to put him in a more comfortable position he clutched eagerly at her dress, as if he felt that the ground was slipping from under him. But the mother, still lost in contemplation of the scene before her, failed to observe this sign of her boy's agitation.

It was noontide. The sun moved slowly through the azure sky. At the foot of the hill swept the swollen river. The ice had broken up, but the turbid stream was flecked with floating bergs, fast melting in the noonday heat. On the flooded meadows the waters had formed mirror-like lakelets, wherein were reflected fleecy clouds, which were wasting as fast as the tiny icebergs in the rolling river. Now and then a gust of wind blew over the meadows, covering the lakelets with ripples which gleamed in the sunlight like molten silver. From the steaming fields on the opposite side of the river floated a diaphanous mist, shrouding in a tremulous veil of white the dark pine trees which bounded the horizon. It seemed as if the earth sighed with gladness, and there rose from its broad bosom the smoke of a sacrificial offering of thanksgiving.

The scene resembled a vast temple prepared for a glorious feast. But for the blind boy it was merely an immense darkness which moved and moaned around him, touching his soul from every side, thrilling him with new and unknown sensations and stirring his heart with unspeakable thoughts.

Instinctively he raised his face to the sun, which warmed his delicate skin, as if he knew that it was the point whither all surrounding nature gravitated. Yet for him the deep azure of the sky, the transparent clearness of the air, the vastness of the horizon, had no existence. He knew only that something warm, something almost solid, was warmly caressing his cheek. And then the caress was swept away by something cool, fresh and lively—something which moved—and for a moment the warmth became no more than a memory.

At home, Petrik had been accustomed to move freely about, knowing that around him was emptiness. But now he felt as if rapidly undulating waves of some strange substance were alternately warming and cooling the air and intoxicating him with a sense of keen delight. The wind which fanned his cheeks whistled in his ears and pressed against his face, his neck and his whole body, as if trying to lift him off his feet and throw him into space. And this mysterious force, these undulating waves, which flowed all round him, were mingled with a thousand different sounds. Now it was the bright song of the soaring skylark, now the soft rustling of the young leaves, now the liquid music of the surging river. The swallow flew past on her lightsome wings, the flies buzzed as they circled round his head, and from time to time the long melancholy cry of a ploughman, as he urged his horses in a far-away field, could be faintly heard.

The boy was unable to bring order out of this anarchy of sounds; he could not co-ordinate them according to perspective, or connect them with definite ideas. They rushed into his dark little head—the soft and the vague, the low and the loud, the gentle and the boisterous—sometimes separately, sometimes crowding together in a grating discord. The wind whistled and hissed in his ears, rising higher and higher until it drowned all minor sounds.

Then it sank again; and it seemed to Petrik that the world which they represented was sinking and dying like the memory of a bygone day. His mind, weak as yet, began to falter under the weight of so many new impressions. For a while he struggled with them; but the task was beyond his strength. The sounds from the encircling darkness whelmed over his soul like the waters of a great flood—sounds now rising, now falling, now once more mingling with the plaintive human cry in the fields over the river.

Then all of a sudden came a deep silence.

It was too much. With a groan Petrik fell back upon the grass. The mother, turning swiftly towards him, uttered a cry of dismay. Her boy was stretched on the ground pale and unconscious.

CHAPTER V.

THE accident, as they called it, which befell the blind boy greatly disturbed Uncle Maxim, none the less so that he dimly divined the cause. He thought it had something to do with the mind, and by way of enlightening his own on the subject, sent for the best books on physiology, pyschology, pedagogy, and what not, which he could obtain, and studied, with his wonted energy, all that might concern the mysterious growth of a child's soul.

Soon the work absorbed him completely, and as the result of his studies and observations he arrived at certain definite conclusions. He saw that though Nature had deprived Petrik of sight, she had bestowed upon him many noble qualities. All his other senses were wonderfully acute. He realized the impressions to which he was susceptible with remarkable fulness and intensity. And Maxim's heart warmed within him at the thought that, maimed though he was, his might be the privilege of lightening his nephew's affliction; that by assiduous effort he might train the blind boy to be a champion of the right and the true, and make him a great and good man.

"Who knows?" soliloquized the old Garibaldian. "It is not with the sword alone that the world's wars are waged. Who knows that in the time to come Petrik will not wield the weapons that are his—speech and thought—for the promotion of his fellow-creatures' happiness, and in defending the helpless and oppressed from tyranny and wrong? Then will a crippled old soldier not have lived in vain."

After the walk to the hillock by the river-side, Petrik was several days confined to his bed, suffering, as it seemed, from nervous shock, alternating with delirium. One moment he would mutter meaningless phrases, the next listen with strained attention to imaginary sounds, his face wearing an expression of anxious perplexity.

"He looks as if he were trying to understand something, and could not," said the mother as she laid her hand on the boy's burning brow.

Maxim, who had been looking pensively on, gave an affirmative nod. He rightly surmised that the child's strange agitation and the swoon were due to the same cause—a flood of impressions too great for his mind, unaided by the sense of sight, to assimilate and digest. It was therefore resolved, on the uncle's proposal, that Petrik should only be exposed to new impressions by slow degrees. To begin with, the double sashes were again put up, and the room resumed its wonted aspect. After a while the windows were occasionally opened for a few minutes at a time, then from morning to night. Next, he was taken into the verandah, and from the verandah into the garden. And Lady Popelsky would explain, with loving patience, the significance of the sounds which perplexed his sensitive ear.

"That strange noise behind the grove," she would

say, "is the shepherd's horn; he is calling his sheep. And there! don't you hear the song of the thrush and the chirping of the sparrows, and the hoarse cry, down there by the river? That is the stork. He is come for the summer, come from a far distant land, and is building his nest in the old place."

And Petrik, taking her hand and nodding his little head, his face beaming with gratitude and pleasure, would listen eagerly and try to understand his mother's explanations.

At the mention of the stork he stretched out his hands, a way he had when trying to realize to himself the relative sizes of things.

"No," said Maxim, "the stork is much bigger than that. If you brought him into the house and placed him on the floor his head would be higher than the back of the chair."

"Ah! a big bird! And a hedge-sparrow is only so," said Petrik, bringing the palms of his hands almost together.

"Yes, dear boy. But big birds never sing so well as little ones. But the stork is a serious bird. He stands in his nest on one leg, looking round and growling like an angry farmer scolding his men, never minding that his voice is hoarse and harsh, and that everybody can hear him."

As he listened to his uncle, the boy, forgetting for a moment his efforts to understand his mother's less vivid descriptions, laughed merrily. Nevertheless, her explanations had a greater charm for him than Maxim's. And when he was troubled or in doubt it was always to her that he addressed his questions. Thus, little by little, Petrik's mind was enriched with new impressions. Striving instinctively and continuously to draw aside the veil of his blindness and see through his mind's eye things invisible, and being gifted with hearing of preternatural acuteness, he comprehended every day more fully the mysterious world into which he had been born. But this incessant strain made him look older than his years and left on his beautiful face the impress of a vague yet profound sadness.

Yet even for the blind boy there were times of unalloyed enjoyment and bright childish pleasure; and when he received impressions which gave him some new emotion, revealing to his mental vision a new aspect of the invisible world, Petrik was supremely happy. It was thus once when they took him to a high cliff, rising abruptly from the river's brink. With beating heart he listened to the tumult of the waters in the depths below, and as a stone, dislodged by his foot, rolled down the cliff and splashed into the river, he clung to his mother in sudden fear. And ever afterwards the idea of depth appeared to his imagination as the soft splashing of water at the foot of a precipice, and stones rolling into a river.

His idea of distance was a song dying away in soft cadences.

When one of the thunderstorms, so frequent in Ruthenia, arose and threatening echoes thundered through the sky, the boy's heart filled with reverent fear, and his mind conceived the grand idea of the vastness of the heavens and the immensity of space.

And so his mental and moral development went on, hardly a day passing that he did not learn something. Before he was six years old he moved freely about in the house without guidance, going whither he listed, and finding without difficulty what he wanted. A stranger, ignorant of his infirmity, would have taken Petrik, not for a blind boy, but for one exceptionally serious and thoughtful, who seemed to be always looking a long way off with strange, motionless eyes.

CHAPTER VI.

ONE fine summer evening Uncle Maxim sat in the garden enveloped, according to his wont, in a cloud of smoke. The father was absent as usual; and in and out of the house there reigned a deep silence. Petrik had been in bed a full half-hour; but as yet, though drowsy, he did not sleep. For several nights past he had experienced strange feelings at this quiet twilight hour. He had fallen asleep with an exquisite sense of delight for which, on wakening in the morning, he was utterly unable to account. At the very moment when his senses were being softly lulled into sweet forgetfulness, and the rustle of the beech trees in the dying breeze, the distant barking of dogs in the village, the trill of the nightingale in the grove, the monotonous tinkle of cattle bells in the pasture were growing fainter and fainter, it seemed to him as if these incongruous sounds, suddenly uniting into a harmonious whole, floated gently through the windows and hovered over his bed, bringing with it heavenly dreams.

And when he woke up at dawn he appeared greatly excited, his first thought being always of these mysterious harmonies of the night.

"What was it? What was it that came through my window last night?" he asked his mother eagerly one morning.

Lady Popelsky, greatly puzzled, was compelled to say that she could not tell him. She had not the remotest idea what it was. But when night came, thinking that her boy was troubled with dreams, she put him to bed herself, only going away when he seemed to be fast asleep, and after piously making the sign of the cross over his head. But in the morning Petrik repeated with much animation the question of the night before.

"Oh, it was so delightful, mamma! But what was it? do tell me what it was."

The mother, being still quite unable to suggest any explanation of the mystery, could only answer that he must have been dreaming; but the next night she resolved to stay with him a little longer, and taking her knitting, sat by his bedside until his regular breathing showed, as she thought, that he slept soundly. All seemed well with him, and Lady Popelsky was stealing quietly from the room when she heard Petrik's voice murmuring her name.

"Mamma, are you here?" he whispered.

"Yes, dear."

"Please go; he is afraid of you. I was nearly asleep, and he has not come."

This mystified Lady Popelsky more than ever. There seemed something uncanny about it all. Petrik was a sensible child, not given to illusions or hallucinations—optical delusions were out of the question. Yet, here he was, speaking of his dreams as something tangible and real, personifying them even. He had not come! She could make nothing of it, and with a sense of growing uneasiness she gave her boy a kiss and went away, only, however, to go into the garden and watch near the open window of her boy's room.

She had not been there many minutes when she found the reading of the riddle. The soft south wind was wafting towards the house the low and sweet, yet hardly audible notes of a flute. It was this simple melody which, reaching Petrick's sensitive ear at the witching time between waking and sleeping, had given him so keen delight and so many happy dreams.

After listening for a moment to the "wood notes wild" of the touching Ruthenian air Lady Popelsky joined Uncle Maxim.

"Tokim plays remarkably well," she said to her brother. "It is surprising to find so much delicacy of feeling in a coarse-looking stable hand."

It was true, Tokim did play well—both flute and fiddle—and there had been a time when only the old and decrepit could hear and sit still when he played one of his more lively measures. They made people dance in spite of themselves.

But after Tokim fell in love with Mary, one of the maids at a neighbouring country house, he exchanged the merry fiddle for the melancholy flute, probably because the faithless fair had jilted him in favour of her master's footman. Since that time the fiddle had hung unused and neglected on a peg in the stable, its strings bursting, one by one, with death cries so piteous that the horses neighed in sympathy and turned their heads wonderingly to their love-lorn groom.

He bought his first flute from a gipsy tinker. It was little more than a rudely-fashioned wooden pipe, so wooden indeed that, try as he might, Tokim could neither make it respond to his feelings nor breathe into it any sort of musical life. He bought a dozen more pipes of the same make. They were all alike. He could not get a satisfactory tune out of the best of them. They whistled when he wanted them to sing, screamed when he wanted them to wail, chirped when he wanted them to sigh, and were altogether unmelodious and unmanageable.

It was evident that no gipsy pipe could be attuned to the feelings of a Ruthenian lover.

So Tokim resolved to make a pipe for himself, and in this intent rambled about the fields and marshes several days, carefully inspecting every willow bush he came across, and now and again cutting away one of the thicker boughs. But he found nothing likely, and was on the point of giving up the quest in despair when he chanced on a reach of the river, where the water was so calm that it hardly stirred the heads of the water lilies which floated on its bosom. It was sheltered from the wind by a thick belt of willow trees, which bent pensively over the lonesome pool. Tokim pushed his way through the brambles; and as he stood for a moment in silent contemplation at the water's edge, his eye brightened and his knitted brows unbent, for here, he felt persuaded, he should find what he had so long vainly sought. Looking round, he spied close beside him a stem which seemed as well suited to his purpose as if it had been grown to order. It was round, smooth, straight and perfectly sound, of the right thickness, with a beautiful silvery bark, and as flawless as a piece of polished marble.

"Just the thing," murmured Tokim, throwing into the water a bundle of boughs which he had previously secured, on the off chance of finding among them a stick that would do. "Just the thing."

Then, with his clasp knife, he severed the chosen stem from the parent tree and took it home. So soon as it was thoroughly dried, he burnt out the pith with a red-hot iron, and with the same tool bored in the tube six round holes. The seventh, which had to be oval, he made with his knife. This done, he stopped the end of the pipe with a wooden plug and laid it outside on a piece of thin lace, where, for a whole week, it was warmed in the sun and fanned by the wind. Next he shaped it with his knife, and polished it with sand-paper and a rough woollen rag. The upper part was round; but from the middle downwards it was cut into smooth, regular facets, on which Tokim had burnt, with small pieces of hot wire, various complicated arabesques.

The flute was made.

Tokim tried a few rapid notes. Then, with an exclamation of pleasure, he hid the instrument under his pillow. He did not want to play his first solo during the bustle of the day. But at nightfall, when he had fed and bedded down his horses, and all was quiet, the stable resounded for an hour or more with sweet and melancholy Ruthenian melodies.

Tokim was more than content with his flute; he was delighted. It seemed to be part of himself. He could do with it what he would. Its music came straight from his own warm and tender heart. Every shade of his feelings, every phase of his sorrow, were breathed into the magic flute, and softly taking wing, flew sonorously through the listening night.

He fell in love with it, and they spent together a happy honeymoon. During the day he attended faithfully to his duties; and sometimes, as he looked towards the house where lived his cruel beauty, he had a spasm of the old heart-ache. But when night came he lost himself in musical ecstasies; his memories of the dark-eyed Mary melted into nothingness, leaving behind them only a vague yearning that gave a charming touch of melancholy to the airs which he drew from his responsive flute.

One evening, not long after his first trial with his new instrument, Tokim lay on his hard bed in a corner of the stable in a paroxysm of musical delight, and oblivious to all earthly things. He had forgotten not merely his false sweetheart but even his own existence when, all of a sudden, he ceased his piping, and, shuddering fearfully, leaped up in blank dismay.

Invisible fingers had brushed his face, and after touching his hands swept lightly over the flute.

A ghost!

"The Holy Cross protect us!" he cried. "Are you from God or the devil?"

Just then a wandering moonbeam shone through the open door, revealing the blind boy, who stood by Tokim's bedside, stretching towards him his tiny hands.

An hour later Lady Popelsky went as usual to

Petrik's chamber to see how he slept and make over his head the sign of the cross.

He was not there, and her heart sank with a sudden fear. Then, remembering where he was likely to be, she left the room and the house, and walked softly towards the stable.

Meanwhile the playing had been resumed; and it continued without intermission until Tokim, chancing to raise his eyes, saw to his confusion that the "noble lady" was standing at the door; and, as might appear, she had been there for some time, enjoying the music and watching her boy, who sat on the bed wrapped in Tokim's cloak and listening delightedly to his melodious piping.

CHAPTER VII.

PETRIK now spent all his evenings in the stables. It never occurred to him to ask Tokim to play at any other time. The day was too garish and noisy for real enjoyment. Moreover, Tokim had his horses to look after. But when the heat and burden of the day were over and the red sun sank behind the black pine woods, Petrik fell into a very fever of impatience, and the supper-bell served only to denote that the longed-for moment was at hand.

Now all this was the reverse of pleasing to Lady Popelsky; yet she could not find it in her heart to prevent her darling from spending an hour or two with Tokim before going to bed. As for Petrik, these hours were the happiest of his life; and his mother saw with growing jealousy that this new-born passion for music possessed her boy all day long. Even when he sat on her lap his thoughts were of Tokim and his flute, and it was plain to see that he did not respond to her caresses with the same fervour as of yore.

As she turned these matters over in her mind, Anna Mikailovna remembered that among the accomplishments which she had acquired in her girlhood, at Madame Radetzky's school for young ladies of the nobility, was some knowledge of music. The thought did not, however, give her any particular satisfaction, being associated with memories of her teacher, Fräulein Klaps, a lean, cross, prosaic German old maid, whose speciality was "breaking up" her pupil's fingers in order to give them proper flexibility. The result was that she generally managed at the same time to deprive these members of all delicacy of touch, and made what ought to have been a pleasure a painful ordeal.

So it came to pass that since she left school Anna Mikailovna had never once touched the piano.

But now, as she listened, jealously brooding, to Tokim's playing, there re-awakened within her that feeling for living melody which Fräulein Klaps's finger-cracking propensities had not sufficed entirely to destroy.

The next day Lady Popelsky asked her husband to buy her a pianoforte.

"Certainly, my dear," answered the good man. "But—I thought you did not care for music."

"I used not to do. But I was thinking that if I had a piano——"

"You might possibly play on it occasionally. And it would be very nice to hear you. I will write to order one this very day, and I promise you it shall be an instrument of high quality."

The order was sent accordingly, but either owing to the long distance which it had to travel, or the stringent stipulations as to quality which Mr. Popelsky had enjoined, the piano did not arrive at the manor house for several weeks.

Meanwhile the flute-playing went on, Petrik betaking himself nightly to the stable, often without so much as asking his mother's leave. He generally sat as if spellbound, listening intently and never interrupting. But one evening, when Tokim stopped for a few minutes, the boy's mute admiration gave place to an unspeakable longing, which he signified by stretching out his hands towards the flute. Tokim gave it to him, and it was no sooner in his hands than he put it eagerly to his lips. His emotion was, however, so great that his breath came in gasps, and the first attempt proved a failure. But when he grew calmer he learnt quickly. Tokim put his pupil's fingers on the holes, and though his hands were too small to stretch an octave he soon knew every tone of the register. His vivid imagination gave to each note a distinct personality. In every hole there dwelt a little sonorous spirit, whose voice he knew. Often when Tokim played some slow melody the boy's fingers moved in unison with those of his master. He realized fully the consecutive notes by their respective positions.

At last, after a month's waiting, the piano arrived.

When Petrik heard the news he went into the courtyard and listened to the unloading and the carrying of the "music" into the house, trying the while to imagine what it was like. It was evidently very heavy, for when it was moved the cart creaked and the men breathed hard and groaned laboriously. When it was on the ground they heaved sighs of relief; and then, lifting the thing up, they walked on with heavy, measured steps, while something inside vibrated, groaned and grumbled, as if it were protesting against being so rudely handled. Stranger still, when this queer instrument was dropped on the drawing-room floor, it emitted a sharp, scolding cry, as if it were threatening everybody with its displeasure.

All this made an unfavourable impression on Petrik. He both feared and disliked the instrument, and going into the garden, remained there while the piano was being put into order by the tuner, who had accompanied it from town.

So soon as all was ready Anna Mikailovna sent for her son. With so fine an instrument, brought expressly from Vienna, she reckoned on an easy victory over the coachman and his flute. Henceforth, she felt sure, he would be left to play his solos in the solitude of his stable, and her dear boy would spend all his evenings with her, as he used to do.

The piano was the magic loadstone which should win him back to his allegiance.

With laughing eyes Lady Popelsky looked fondly at Petrik, then significantly at Maxim, as much as to say, "Wait a minute and you will see."

Last of all, she threw a glance of pitying condescension at poor Tokim, who had begged leave to listen to the "foreign music," and stood humbly at the door.

And then, after a little preliminary flourish, to show that her hand had not lost its cunning, she began.

The chosen piece was one she had learned to perfection at Madame Radetzky's school. Though not particularly loud, it was rather difficult, requiring on the part of the player considerable mechanical skill. At the public examination the successful performance of this piece won Anna Mikailovna great applause, and Fräulein Klaps was warmly congratulated on her pupil's brilliant execution. It was even said that her rendering of this particular piece had won the silent Popelsky's heart. Now she was playing it with the set purpose of regaining her boy's heart, which she thought had been stolen from her by Tokim's pipe.

But this time, instead of victory, she found defeat. The grand piano from Vienna could not compete with the Ruthenian flute, and in Petrik's opinion the lady pianist was no match for the humble piper.

True, her thin fingers were nimbler and quicker than Tokim's heavy digits; the airs she played were richer and more complex than his, and she kept most excellent time. But the harmonious groom was a born musical genius.

He had loved and suffered, and he breathed into his flute all the poetry of his soul. He learnt his simple melodies from the rustling of the forest, the soft whisperings of the grass on the steppes and the airs of the pathetic Ruthenian ballads, which had been sung over his very cradle.

Anna Mikailovna had hardly begun her concerto, which she flattered herself she was doing exceedingly well, when the hasty tapping of Maxim's stick on the carpet told her that something was wrong. Turning her head, she saw on Petrik's pale face the same agonized look which it wore on the day of his first walk in the early spring, when he fell senseless on the grass.

Tokim looked pityingly at the blind boy; then, casting a contemptuous glance at the "foreign music," he left the room, and the next moment his great boots were thumping on the floor and resounding through the hall.

This mortifying fiasco caused the poor mother much heart-searching and many tears. At first she was highly indignant. The thought that she, a noble lady, whose playing had been applauded by a select audience of her own class, had been ignominiously beaten by a common stable-boy, was almost more than she could bear, and in her anger she denounced Tokim as a coarse, low-bred, unfeeling knave.

Nevertheless, when her son left her side for the groom's more congenial society, she always sat at the window, listening intently, and trying to persuade herself that the flute-playing was nothing more than the foolish twittering of a peasant's pipe. But after a while the foolish twittering took such hold of her that she forgot the piper in his piping, and paid his touching melodies the tribute of involuntary admiration. And then she asked herself wherein lay the attraction of these improvisations, the charm of which she was unable to withstand. After long musing she found the answer, found it in the blue evening sky, in the ghostly shadows of the night, in the sighing of the wind through the trees. The charm of Tokim's melodies lay in their very simplicity, their harmony with surrounding nature.

"Yes, it must be so," she thought, for the first time seeing and acknowledging the truth. "In Tokim's playing there is something quite peculiar; he has genuine poetic feeling, and a sympathy with nature which find their manifestation in beautiful music that speaks to the heart. He has mastered the secret; while I—I have neither musical gifts nor true poetic feeling."

And Anna Mikailovna fell a weeping, oblivious to the fact that, though she might not possess Tokim's musical genius, she had feelings as true and deep as his. If the groom had an ardent love for nature, she had a stronger, holier love—a mother's love for the blind boy who deserted her for another because she could not charm his soul with the same sweet melodies.

In truth, the sense of her boy's blindness was so acute, her pity for him so tender, her yearning for his love so impassioned, that it made her physically ill, rendering her morbidly sensitive to every sign of his affliction and anxious beyond expression about his future. This strange rivalry with the peasant musician, which to most women would have been a mere annoyance, became to her a source of burning sorrow.

Time, though for a while it brought her no sensible relief, at length gave a new turn to her thoughts. She began to feel within herself something of that living sense of poetry and melody which so charmed her in Tokim's playing. Then her hopes revived; and, stirred by her naturally high courage, she several times went to the piano, intent on silencing with its richer notes the more modest music of Tokim's flute, only, however, to be restrained by a feeling of bashful irresolution from carrying out her design. She could not forget Petrik's pain-stricken face and the groom's contemptuous glance, and her hands swept over the key-board in timid hesitation.

Yet every day the consciousness of her strength

increased. Whenever Petrik took a walk or played in the park she practised assiduously—for a while, however, with little satisfaction to herself. She could not make her fingers respond to her thoughts. The sounds she produced seemed foreign to her feelings. But this difficulty she gradually mastered; and there came a time when she felt capable of expressing her emotions with comparative fulness and ease.

Tokim's lessons and her own maternal instinct had taught Anna Mikailovna how to win back her boy's heart.

Soon she felt strong enough to enter the lists openly, and one evening there took place a singular contest—nothing less than a pitched battle between the great lady and the harmonious groom. From the dark coach-house, with its low thatched roof, floated the soft tremulous music of the silvery flute, while from the open windows of the drawing-room, gleaming through the beech trees, rushed the fuller and richer strains of the grand piano.

At first neither Petrik nor Tokim gave heed to this aggressive demonstration of the competing instrument. But after a while the boy grew angry and impatient, and the old look came over his face.

Suddenly Tokim stopped playing.

"Go on! Why don't you go on?" exclaimed the boy.

"Listen!" said Tokim softly, and Petrik listened.

The next night and the night after the contest was resumed, and every now and then the groom would lay aside his flute and listen with ever-growing delight. During the pauses Petrik listened too, and with so much interest that he forgot to urge his friend to continue. On the third night Tokim put down his flute, saying pensively:

"How nice it is! Who would have thought it?"

Then, with the absent air of a listening man, he took Petrik's hand, and the two, walking softly through the garden, stood in the shadow of a beech tree, near the drawing-room window.

Tokim imagined that the "noble lady" was playing solely for her own amusement and knew not that they were listening. But Anna Mikailovna's quick ear told her that the flute-playing had ceased, and, guessing what had happened, her heart overflowed with joy. This time, at least, the victory was hers. A grand victory; a victory without bitterness. Her anger against Tokim had long since disappeared, and now she was fain to acknowledge that she owed her new-born happiness entirely to him. It was he who had taught her how to gain her child's heart; she could now unfold to him a world of new impressions. For this great blessing they were indebted to their common teacher and friend, the peasant piper.

The ice was broken. On the following morning Petrik entered the drawing-room with timid curiosity, for the first time since the eventful day when the strange guest from Vienna, who had seemed to him so choleric and boisterous, arrived at the manor house.

But the performance of the night before had won his admiration and wrought a complete change in his feelings.

Petrik crept furtively towards the piano; then, coming to a dead stop, listened intently.

There was nobody in the room. But through the open door of an adjoining room his mother was watching him with bated breath, marking his every movement and observing every change that passed over his beautiful mobile face.

Stretching out his hands, Petrik touched the polished surface of the walnut case, then fell back. After several times repeating this experiment he drew nearer, and felt the piano all over. When he had formed definite ideas as to its size and shape, he laid his fingers lightly on the keyboard and a soft, hesitating sound trembled in the air.

The boy listened eagerly to the delicate vibrations long after they had become inaudible to his mother. With the same close attention he touched another key. Then, passing his hand over the whole keyboard, he sounded several notes of the higher register. To every note he gave sufficient time, making it vibrate, tremble and die out, his face meanwhile bespeaking deep interest and keen delight. He was evidently admiring and studying each separate tone, proving by this spontaneous appreciation of the elements of melody that he had in him the making of a true artist.

His manner, moreover, showed that he ascribed to each tone peculiar qualities. When his fingers touched some gay and brilliant note of the higher register he would lift his lively face upward, as if that were the direction which the fugitive had taken. But when he struck one of the lower keys he would bend his ear downwards, as if he thought that so heavy a sound had fallen on the floor and was dying out in distant corners.

CHAPTER VIII.

Uncle Maxim did not regard these musical experiments with unalloyed satisfaction.

Petrik's passion for music produced in the old Garibaldian a double feeling. Though pleased that his nephew appeared to possess exceptional gifts, he would have been much better pleased if his bent had been in some other direction. In other words, he was disappointed.

"I know," he said to himself, "I know that music is a power. It touches people's hearts. In the time to come Petrik will gather round him crowds of applauding idlers, men and women, and play for them all sorts of waltzes and nocturnes (obviously Maxim's ideas of music were somewhat limited), and they will wipe away foolish tears with perfumed pocket handkerchiefs .... Ah! This is not what I expected from him. But what is to be done? The poor little chap is blind and must do the best he can."

In accordance with the educational scheme adopted by Maxim, Petrik continued to be left as much as possible to his own devices. The result was in every way satisfactory. He walked about the house freely and unguided, kept his room in order, and himself took care of his playthings and other belongings.

Nor was his physical education neglected. He had his own gymnasium and a well-broken, well-mannered little pony, given to him by his uncle on his sixth birthday. When it was first mooted to her, Lady Popelsky would not listen to the mad idea, as she deemed it, of her blind child riding on horseback. But Maxim, as he generally did in the end, got his own way; and in two or three months Petrik was galloping merrily about on his pony under the guidance of Tokim, who never, however, except when it was necessary to turn, or avoid an obstruction, interfered with the freedom of his movements.

So it came to pass that the boy's infirmity was no hindrance to wholesome bodily growth, and Maxim did his utmost to minimize its influence on the moral side of his nephew's nature.

At this time Petrick was slightly built, yet tall

for his age; his face had little colour and his features were delicate and expressive. His black hair matched well with his pale skin and large dark eyes which, as they seldom moved, gave him a strange, almost uncanny look, that always attracted the attention of those who saw him for the first time. This peculiarity, together with a slight wrinkling of the brows, a habit of bending the head a little forward, and a shade of sadness which ever and anon flitted over his beautiful face, were the sole outward signs of his blindness.

In a place which he knew Petrik's movements were bold and confident, yet those who watched him closely could easily see, by his general manner and an occasional nervous gesture, that the fact of his infirmity sensibly modified the natural vivacity of his temper.

As time went on music became more and more the chief interest and occupation of the blind boy's life. He learnt, with no more trouble than listening to them attentively, the airs which were

THE BLIND MUSICIAN.   63

played or sung in his hearing, and caught easily
the voices of surrounding nature. These he would
often unite into one by a free improvisation, in
which, however, it was difficult to draw the line
between the popular melody and the personal
creation. So closely were the two elements inter-
mingled in his mind that even himself could not
always distinguish the original from the acquired.

Although Petrik took kindly to the piano, and
learnt readily everything which he practised with
his mother, he did not abandon Tokim's pipe.
The piano was richer, fuller and louder, but it
had the disadvantage of being always in the same
place, while the flute could be taken out of doors
and played to the accompaniment of the wild
music of the steppe and the mystic murmurings
of the forest.

When Petrik was nine years old, Maxim, who
had meanwhile studied assiduously the best methods
of instructing the blind, taught him to read and
gave him a regular course of lessons. The boy

proved an apt pupil and made rapid progress; and this training, besides providing him with a multitude of new ideas and new pleasures, corrected that proneness to introspection and dreaminess which was the natural outcome of his blindness and his passion for music.

The blind boy's days were thus well filled, and he had no lack of varied impressions. He lived as full a life as was possible for a boy of his age, and seemed to have no consciousness—at any rate painful consciousness—of his infirmity. Nevertheless, there was perceptible in his character an unchildish sadness, and his ways were not as the ways of other children. Maxim ascribed this peculiarity to the fact of Petrik having no young companions, and tried to find an antidote for the bane.

Peasant boys of the neighbourhood were asked to the manor house and bidden to play with Petrik. But abashed by their unwonted surroundings and the blindness of their young host, the lads seemed ill at ease. They herded together and kept timidly silent, or talked to each other in whispers. When let out into the garden or the park they played heartily and enjoyed themselves; but on these occasions Petrick was left out in the cold, listening sorrowfully to the merry shouts of his comrades.

At other times he would gather them round him and tell them amusing stories, which the lads, who were well acquainted with Ruthenian folk lore and had heard strange things of warlocks, witches and the devil, would cap with stories of their own. Hence these entertainments were often very lively, yet Petrik, albeit he listened with attention, seldom laughed, the humour of spoken words, like many other things, being beyond the blind boy's ken. And no wonder, the narrator's laughing eyes and whimsical gestures were alike invisible to him.

Now, a short time before Maxim's attempt to find a remedy for his nephew's melancholy, there came to live in the neighbourhood a married couple, of the name of Yakutsky. They were no longer young, their united ages making a total of nearly a century. Nevertheless, they had not been long married. Mr. Yakutsky, albeit a gentleman born, had to struggle hard and long in order to scrape together capital enough to buy and stock a farm. All this time he remained a bachelor; while his sweetheart, to whom he was betrothed while still a young man, lived as lady companion in the house of the Countess Sadova. When, at length, they felt themselves justified in marrying, her face had lost the bloom of youth and his scanty locks were silvered with age. But their hearts were as young as ever and they were very happy; all the more so as shortly after our blind boy came into the world, God gave them a little girl. She was a sweet child with fair hair and blue eyes, and struck all who saw her by the peculiar gravity of her face and the self-possession of her manners. It seemed as if the sobriety of a tardy union were reflected in the girl's character—in her unchildlike reasonableness—in the quietness of her movements and in her deep blue eyes. She showed no shyness with strangers, and was always at home with grown-up people. On the other hand, she did not avoid the company of children, sometimes even playing with them. But she joined in their sports with a certain condescension, as if it were rather for their amusement than for her pleasure. What this little girl liked best, however, was to wander about alone, gathering flowers and talking to her doll, but with an aptness and seriousness more befitting a diminutive woman than a young girl.

CHAPTER IX.

ONE fine afternoon Petrik strolled to his favourite mound by the river.

The sun was setting, the air was still. Petrik sat down and produced his flute, now an inseparable companion. After playing a while he laid it aside, and stretching himself on the grass, listened to the lowing of the cattle as they wended homeward from the fields, the sweet song of the soaring skylark and the twilight hum of invisible insects, enjoying to the full the drowsy languor of the summer evening.

In the midst of his reverie he hears the sound of light footsteps. Vexed at being disturbed he raises himself on his elbow and listens. The footsteps are coming up the mound, and as they are unfamiliar to him he knows that the intruder is a stranger.

The next moment he hears a girl's voice.

"Boy," it says, "could you tell me who was playing the flute just now?"

"It was I," he gruffly answers the disturber of his solitude.

"Oh!" exclaims the girl. Then, in a tone of ingenuous approbation, she adds:

"You play very well."

"Why don't you go your way?" is Petrik's ungallant reply.

"But why do you want me to go away?" asks the other wonderingly.

Her sweet low voice soothes Petrik's ear, yet he says in the same tone as before:

"I don't like people to come here."

"You don't like people to come here!" says the child with an amused laugh. "Why, I should like to know? One might think all the world belonged to you, and nobody was to walk on it but yourself."

"Mother said I was not to be disturbed."

"And my mother said I might walk by the river whenever I liked."

On this, Petrik, who is not used to be contradicted, flies into a passion.

"Go! go! go!" he exclaims angrily, at the same time rising to his feet.

As the girl, quite taken aback by this outburst, regards him in blank surprise, Tokim's voice is heard calling Petrik to tea, who thereupon runs swiftly down the hill with the little woman's indignant exclamation, "Oh, what a bad boy!" ringing in his ears.

The next evening Petrik went to the mound again, all his anger gone, and even wishing that the girl with the silvery voice might pass his way again. The children whom he knew were rude and boisterous, shouting uproariously with voices which grated on his sensitive ear. None spoke so pleasantly as she. Yet he greatly feared that he had so offended her that she would come no more.

Neither did she—on that evening—but he went again and again in the same hope, and on the fourth evening, as he lay on the grass in silent expectation, he heard her footfall down by the river. She was walking slowly, humming a song, and pushing the pebbles about with her feet.

"Hallo! is that you?" called Petrik as she came nearer. The girl went on singing, the pebbles continued to roll under her feet, and there was something in her voice which told Petrik that his rudeness still rankled in her mind.

But when she drew near she ceased her singing and came to a stand, as if to arrange the wild flowers which she had been gathering down by the river.

Taking this long pause as a sign of assumed indifference, Petrik waited patiently for an answer.

"Don't you see that it is I?" said the girl at last with great dignity.

A simple question enough; yet it jarred painfully on the blind boy's ear. He answered nothing, but the hand on which he rested closed nervously on a bunch of grass. Nevertheless, the acquaintance was made.

"Who taught you to play the flute?" asked the girl, still keeping her distance.

"Tokim."

"And you play very well. But why are you so cross?"

"I—I am not cross," said Petrik deprecatingly.

"Neither am I. Shall we play together?"

"I don't know how to play," returned Petrik, bowing his head.

"Don't know how to play! Well, I never! But why?"

"Because——"

"Well! Why don't you know how to play? Tell me, please."

"Because——" said Petrik in a hardly audible whisper, bowing his head still lower.

Never before had he spoken to a stranger about his blindness; the girl's innocent and persistent curiosity touched him to the quick.

"How awkward you are!" she said with an air of patronizing superiority, seating herself by his side. "You say so because you don't know me. When we know each other better you won't be afraid of me in the least—not in the least. I am afraid of nobody."

She spoke with great unconcern, giving little

heed to Petrik, and toying the while with her flowers.

"Where did you gather those flowers?" he asked.

"There!" said the little maid, moving her head.

"In the field?"

"No, there!"

"In the grass, then. What flowers are they?"

"Don't you know? Dear me! What a strange boy you are!"

Petrik took one of the flowers and passed his fingers over the leaves and the corolla.

"This is a buttercup," he said, "and this a violet." Then, wanting to know his new friend as he knew the flowers, he put his left hand round her waist and passed his right softly over her hair, brows and face, dwelling on them for a moment in order to impress her features on his mind.

All this was done so suddenly and swiftly that his surprised companion could not utter a word.

She could only stare at him with large wondering eyes. And then it struck her for the first time that there was something very strange about this new playmate of hers. The pale, delicate features and the knitted brows wore a look of intentness in striking contrast with those awfully motionless eyes, which passively reflected the red glare of the setting sun. As she gazed into those sightless orbs her amazement passed rapidly into something like horror.

By a quick movement she freed herself from his embrace, and springing to her feet, burst into tears.

"Why do you frighten me by looking like that, you wicked boy?" she sobbed passionately; "what have I done to you?"

Petrik was too much surprised, too deeply grieved to answer. He sat still, his head bowed, his heart well nigh bursting with anger and humiliation. For the first time in his life he felt the reproach of his infirmity, and learnt that it could inspire, not pity merely, but repulsion and fear.

A sense of burning wrong and passionate grief contracted his throat until he felt like to choke. Pride prompted him to maintain his dignity; but his feelings were too much for him, and after a wild outburst of tears he threw himself on the ground in a very agony of grief, sobbing bitterly.

On hearing these portentous sounds the little woman, who by this time was running down the hill, turned back in amaze. When she saw Petrik's grief her heart melted and her anger was turned away.

"Listen to me! Why do you cry?" she said, bending down to him. "Perhaps you are afraid that I shall complain. Don't cry. I shall tell nobody—nobody."

These words of sympathy, and the sweetness with which they were spoken, made poor Petrik sob all the more, and he could not answer a word.

The little maid, seating herself beside him, looked on a few minutes in perplexed silence. Then she smoothed his hair and caressed his cheeks, and raising his head with the gentle persistency of a mother soothing a repentant child, took from her pocket a tiny handkerchief and wiped away his tears.

"Enough! enough!" she said in the authoritative tone of a full-grown woman. "That will do. I am not angry with you at all now that I see how sorry you are for having frightened me."

"I did not mean to frighten you," answered Petrik, sighing deeply in the effort to stifle a rising sob.

"Come, now! Don't I tell you that I am not angry. I know you won't do it again. Come, now! I shall not let you lie there any longer. Sit here, near me," laying her hand on his shoulder and rousing him.

Petrik did as he was bidden; but when the little maid looked at his face again she felt almost as much afraid as before. His cold, motionless eyes, wide open to the blinding sunlight, were full of tears, his pale features wrung as with suppressed grief.

"How—very strange—you are still," she said dubiously, holding him at arm's length.

Poor Petrik made a piteous gesture.

"I am not strange," he said; "I am blind."

"Blind!" she murmured in a quavering voice, as if the terrible word whispered by her companion had inflicted on her small womanly heart a grievous wound.

"Blind!" she repeated in an almost inaudible voice, and then, as if unable to express in words the intensity of her compassion, threw her arms round the blind boy's neck and pressed her face to his. All the little woman's anger disappeared on the instant, and like the dear child she was she fell a-weeping and mingled her tears with Petrik's.

For a while both remained silent.

The girl was the first to recover her composure, though her face was very sorrowful and she sighed deeply. With tear-dimmed eyes she watched the flaming sun as he dipped towards the dark horizon. The golden edge of the great ball of fire glistened for the last time, a corruscation of sparks shot up into the sky, and the sombre silhouette of the forest loomed in the distance like a mighty cloud stretching from earth to heaven.

The evening quiet, the gentle breeze that came up from the river and, above all, the warmth and tenderness of his companion's sympathy, soothed Petrik's agitated mind and restored his courage.

"It is because I am so sorry for you," said the little maid with a half sob; and then, mastering her emotion and thinking it would be well to give a new turn to the conversation, she observed that the sun had set.

"I don't know what the sun is like; I only feel it," was the sad rejoinder.

"You don't know the sun?"

"No."

"And your mother! Don't you know her either?"

"Oh, yes, I know my mother; I feel her coming when she is ever so far off."

"So do I. I should know my mother though I could not see her."

After this the talk became quite childlike and confidential.

"Do you know," said Petrik briskly, "do you know that, though I cannot feel the sun, I know when it has set."

"Really! But how?"

"Because, you know. . . . It is like this —I feel it; I tell in that way."

"Oh, yes, I understand," said she, quite satisfied with this explanation.

"And I can read," went on Petrik proudly, "and I am going to learn to write with a pen."

"Read! You! But that——" and then she

checked herself as if fearing to hurt his feelings by too much questioning.

"You wonder how I can read. Well, I read from my own books, with my fingers."

"With your fingers? I am sure I should never learn to read with my fingers. It is as much as I can do to read with my eyes. My father says women are not clever at learning things."

"I read French too."

"How clever you are!" said the little maid in sincere admiration. "But if you stay here I fear you will catch cold. A fog is gathering down there by the river."

"And you?"

"Oh, I am not afraid. Nothing ever hurts me."

"Neither am I. And boys don't take cold as soon as girls. They are stronger. Uncle Maxim says that a man should fear nothing, neither cold, nor hunger, nor thunder, nor rain."

"Maxim! Do you mean the gentleman with crutches? I have seen him. He is awful."

"Oh, no. He is not awful. He is very good."

"No! He is awful, I tell you, simply awful," she repeated firmly. "You don't know because you have not seen him."

"I know him though. He teaches me everything."

"Does he beat you?"

"Never; he does not even scold me."

"Who could? It would be a shame to misuse a blind boy."

"But he never misuses anybody," answered Petrik rather absently. His quick ear had caught Tokim's footsteps on the pebbles, and the next moment the groom came in sight, and his voice was heard calling his young master.

"You are wanted," said the girl rising.

"Yes, but I would rather stay with you here."

"No. You had better go. I will come to see you to-morrow. Now you are expected at home. So am I."

CHAPTER X.

THE little maid kept her promise to the letter. On the following morning, while Petrik was busy with his lessons with Uncle Maxim, the lad suddenly raised his head, listened intently for a moment, and then said with great vivacity:

"Will you let me go out for a few minutes, uncle? The girl is there."

"What girl," asked Maxim with a wondering smile. And then he let Petrik go, following him to the hall door.

Meanwhile, Petrik's new friend had come into the courtyard, and seeing there Lady Popelsky, went boldly, yet modestly, up to her.

"What do you want, my dear?" asked Lady Popelsky, thinking the child had some message to deliver.

"Does a blind boy live here?" asked the small woman, offering her hand with quiet dignity.

"Yes, dear," answered Lady Popelsky, quite charmed with the girl's bright eyes and frank, open manner.

"My mother said I might come. May I see him?"

"And your name is——?"

"Velia Yakutsky."

"Ah! Well, Velia——"

Just then the hall door opened and Petrik ran to greet his visitor, followed—at a considerable distance—by his uncle, whose crutches did not move so quickly as the lad's legs.

"It is the girl I told you about, mother," said Petrik, taking his friend's hand; "but then I have my lessons."

"Never mind. I daresay your uncle will excuse you this morning; I will ask him."

When Velia saw Maxim stumping along with his crutches she went to meet him, and they shook hands.

"It is very good of you not to beat the

blind boy," she observed in a tone of kindly approbation. "I thought you might; but he says you don't."

"Does he?" asked the veteran with playful gravity, holding in his broad palm the girl's tiny hand. "Does he? I am truly grateful to my pupil for securing me the good opinion of so charming a young lady."

And the old cynic, letting go her hand, laughed pleasantly, for the child's blue eyes and engaging ways had quite won his heart.

"Take care, Annie," he said aside to his sister with a significant smile. "Our Petrik is beginning soon, don't you think? And don't you think that, considering his blindness, he has made a very creditable choice? Many who can see make a worse."

"What do you mean, Max?" asked the sister sharply, and a wave of warm blood suffused her face.

"Nothing. I was only joking," said Maxim

with assumed indifference, for he saw that he had given Lady Popelsky pain, quite unintentionally, by speaking the thought which had risen spontaneously in her mind, as in his own.

Anna Mikailovna, blushing still more deeply, and, it may be, dimly foreseeing the future, clasped Velia tenderly in her arms and kissed her passionately, and albeit her eyes widened in mild surprise, the little woman received the great lady's unexpected embrace with her wonted gravity.

From this time forth the intercourse between the manor house and the cottage became close and frequent. Hardly a day passed that Velia did not pay Petrik a visit, and as he never seemed quite happy without her, Lady Popelsky and Maxim invited her to come every day and join in his lessons.

When, however, this plan was broached to Mr. Yakutsky he did not receive it with the satisfaction which might have been expected. To begin with, he held very decided views as to what is called the higher education of women. He thought that a woman who can make an inventory of the household linen and keep a cash account is quite as highly educated as she ought to be. Moreover, being a good Catholic and regarding Garibaldi and all who had fought under his banner as little better than infidels and heretics, he looked on Maxim as a very undesirable teacher for his little daughter. Also, he had heard a fearful rumour that Maxim read Voltaire; and to read Voltaire was worse than to fight against the Austrians and defy the Pope.

But when he had made Maxim's acquaintance he saw reason to modify his views of that gentleman's character. He did not find the devil nearly so black as he was painted. In other words, the arch-heretic and ex-rebel proved to be a very agreeable gentleman of polished manners and great intelligence, who during the whole of their conversation, which had reference in the first place to Velia and Petrik, neither disparaged the Holy Father nor quoted Voltaire.

In these circumstances Mr. Yakutsky, who was as anxious to oblige Lady Popelsky as he was desirous not to offend Maxim, came to the conclusion that he might accept their proposal without exposing his daughter to the risk of perdition. Nevertheless there was a risk, and in the child's interest and his own he deemed it only right to do all that lay in his power to minimize it; so when the time came for Velia's first lesson he took her to the manor house himself, and before leaving. made a solemn little speech, which though spoken to the pupil was meant for the master.

"Listen, my Velia," he began, laying his hand on the girl's shoulder, but looking at Maxim; "listen to what I am about to say, and remember, my child, remember always that there is a God in heaven and a holy pope at Rome. It is I, your father, Valentine Yakutsky, who tell you this, and you must believe me, *primo* (here the dear old gentleman paused for a moment, as if to call Maxim's attention to the fact that he could quote

Latin as well as other folks), *primo*, because I am your father; *secundo*, because I am a nobleman on whose escutcheon is emblazoned not only a crow on a haystack but a cross on a blue field. All the Yakutskys, besides being good and brave knights, have had knowledge of heavenly things. For the rest, touching *orbis terrarum*, which means earthly things, you will listen to Mr. Maxim and—don't be idle."

"You may put your mind at ease," said Maxim with an amused smile. "We do not turn young ladies into Garibaldians."

The new departure proved in every way satisfactory. Both the pupils made good progress, and though Petrik was the more advanced the difference between them was not so great as to exclude healthy emulation. He helped Velia with her lessons and she, on her part, was often able to explain to him things which his blindness rendered it difficult for him to realize or grasp. Moreover, her companionship gave to his studies a savour and a charm which they had hitherto lacked.

In short, this friendship was simply a godsend for the lad. He no longer lost himself in reveries and sought lonesome places. He had found the sympathy and fellowship for which he had so long yearned, and which neither full-grown people nor the children whom he had previously met could give him. Velia's presence was always grateful to him. Their favourite trysting place in fine weather was still the breezy hillock by the river's bank. There she would listen by the hour to Petrik's playing with guileless admiration, and when he laid down his flute she would try to convey to him, in vivid childish metaphors, her impressions of the sights around them. Her very intonations lent force to her words, and through the sense which he possessed to perfection, enabled Petrik to image to himself the scenes which she described. When she spoke of the dark night shrouding the whole earth he seemed to hear darkness in the low silvery accents of her voice. When, lifting up her face she would say:

"Ah! What a dark cloud that is, gathering over there! So dark and heavy!" he would shiver as with cold, and in the inflection of her voice, hear, as it were, a portentous monster crawling across the sky, far, far above their heads.

CHAPTER XI.

THERE be persons in the world whose innate capacity for love and self-sacrifice marks them out as the heroes and heroines of common life, persons to whom care for their kind is like the air they breathe, an organic necessity of their existence. Nature endows these exceptional beings with the calmness of temper and purity of soul which are the essential conditions of spontaneous, every-day magnanimity. Their desire for personal happiness and the pleasures of sense appears to be purposely blunted in order that their passions may be made subservient to the dominant needs of their characters. To superficial observers or casual acquaintances people of this stamp often appear undemonstrative and unfeeling; as free from fleshly lusts as if they were icicles, as devoted to duty as if it were the way to the greatest happiness. Though sympathy and self-abnegation are to them as the bread of life, they seem to the thoughtless as cold as the radiant peaks of the high Alps, and are equally grand. Vulgarity crawls abashed from their feet, even slander touches them not, falling from their stainless robes as foul water falls from the snow-white wings of the swan.

Velia had one of those rare and noble natures which, like genius, is bestowed only on the elect, and, like genius, manifests itself at an early age.

Anna Mikailovna understood what a priceless treasure her blind boy had found in the friendship of this pure-souled girl. So did Uncle Maxim. He thought that his nephew had now all that he needed, and that his moral and intellectual development would proceed smoothly and rapidly, and without drawback.

In this conclusion he was seriously mistaken. Maxim imagined that during the boy's early years —the plastic period of his life—his spiritual development would be under his teacher's control, that he might mould Petrik's mind as he wished.

But when the pupil entered the critical time between childhood and youth, the teacher was fain to acknowledge the vanity of his pedagogic dreams. Almost every week brought to his notice something quite unexpected, which puzzled and confounded him.

One morning Petrik came to his mother in a state of great excitement.

"Mother! mother!" he cried, "I have seen a dream."

"Seen! seen! What can you have seen, my dear boy?" she asked sadly.

"I have had a dream, and I saw you and Uncle Maxim and——"

"What?"

"I cannot remember."

"And me? Don't you remember me?"

The boy's brows knitted painfully, and he made a great effort to recall the impressions of the night. In vain!

"No; I have forgotten it all—all," he answered with a mournful gesture. "Yet I have seen you, I am sure I have—sure, mother."

And then the subject dropped.

Another time, Maxim from the garden heard some strange musical exercises going on in the drawing-room, where Petrik was wont to take his music lessons. The exercise consisted in the playing of two notes only—first a high note, rapidly repeated so as to form an uninterrupted ding, then a bass note, played in the same fashion and producing a like effect. Wondering what all this could mean, Maxim made his way across the garden and entered the house. But on reaching the drawing-room door he stopped short in blank amaze.

Petrik, then in his tenth year, sat on a low stool at his mother's feet. Beside him, stretching out his long neck and swaying monotonously to and fro, stood a tame stork, of which Tokim some time previously had made his young master a present. Every morning Petrik fed the bird with his own hand, and it accompanied him on all his walks. He was now holding the creature with one hand and passing the other slowly and softly over its neck and body, his whole face bespeaking rapt attention. At the same time the mother, bending over the boy with flushed cheeks and sparkling eyes, was repeating the ringing treble note. When Petrik's hand, gliding over the stork's white feathers, reached the black tips of the wings, Lady Popelsky would pass abruptly to the opposite end of the keyboard and strike one of the deepest of the bass notes.

Both mother and son were so absorbed in their singular occupation that neither of them noticed Maxim until, recovering from his surprise, he went forward into the room.

"Anna, what on earth does this mean?" he asked.

Lady Popelsky reddened and looked as confused as if she had been a naughty school-girl caught in *flagrante delicto*.

"Well, you see, Maxim," she began apologetically, "Petrik says he can feel a certain difference in the colouring of the stork's plumage; but he cannot tell in what the difference consists. I assure you it was he who first suggested the idea, and I really think there is something in it."

"Still, I don't quite see——"

"Wait a moment. Well, I wanted to explain to him the difference in colouring by different musical sounds. Don't think it foolish, Max—I really think there is some analogy."

Maxim was so much struck by the originality of the idea that he asked his sister to continue the experiment. But he observed with anxiety the boy's rapt look; and when the brother and sister were alone he shook his head dubiously.

"Listen, Anna," he said. "It is no use raising in Petrik's mind questions which he will never be able to answer——"

"But it was his own suggestion; I had not the least idea," interrupted Lady Popelsky.

"No matter; we have to look at things as they are. The boy is blind, and must be accustomed to his blindness. I mean we must not let him repine; and to that end the less he thinks about it and the less we talk about light and so forth the better. I want to train him so that he will no more regret the deprivation of one of his five senses than we regret the absence of a sixth."

The sister submitted, as she always did, to her brother's stronger will and superior judgment. But this time Maxim was wrong; it was as impossible to suppress the boy's vague yearnings after light as to satisfy them.

Somebody has said that the eyes are the mirrors of the soul. They might be more truly described as the soul's windows, through which enter into it the bright, many-coloured impressions of the outer world. Who can estimate the extent to which our spiritual life depends on our optical impressions?

Now in Petrik's case these windows were hermetically sealed—had, in fact, never been opened. His whole life had to be passed in darkness; yet the potential capacity for optical perception was unimpaired, and existed in full force. He was merely one intermediary link in the endless chain of lives, and that power to see, though during his life it might remain dormant, was capable of being transmitted through him from past to future generations. His soul was a whole human soul with all its faculties.

Hence Petrik's cravings for light were natural and inevitable, and may be likened to that longing to fly, which every imaginative child at some time in its life feels, and which gives rise to so many delightful dreams.

Hence, also, those spontaneous workings of the boy's mind from which his face derived its look of pained perplexity. Inherent, albeit unused, optical capacities moved in his consciousness like so many formless phantoms, goading him to renewed efforts as hopeless as they were distressing.

As time went on, the natural liveliness of his temper became overshadowed by a vague yet persistent melancholy which grew with his years. The laughter which, in his childhood, new and striking impressions had never failed to evoke, was now seldom heard. All of wit and humour and fun that reach the consciousness through the windows of the soul were beyond his ken. The blind boy was as much shut out from these sources of enjoyment as if he lived in a sunless planet. On the other hand, he assimilated with singular fulness the sadness and pathos which abound in the characters, the songs and the folklore of Ruthenian Russia

It was in the nature of things that every intrusion into that darkened soul should give pain, every strange voice jar on it like a dissonant note. True communion of mind is possible only between kindred spirits, and, as we know, Petrik had but one friend of his own age, the fair girl from the cottage.

Their friendship strengthened with time, and was fruitful for both of them. If Velia brought into their relations her calmness of soul and tranquil cheerfulness, and gave to Petrik new conceptions of life he, on his part, made her the confidant of his troubles and the sharer of his inmost thoughts. On the day when he first told her of his blindness the little maid's tender heart received a grievous wound, from which, if the knife that gave it were drawn, she would bleed to death. It was on the lonely hillock of the steppe that she felt for the first time in her life the keen pang of sympathy, and with each succeeding year the blind boy's society became more necessary for her mental peace. If she did not see him for several days the wound would re-open, and she would hasten to her friend and find in her solicitude for him a sovereign balm for her own sufferings.

One warm autumn evening the families were assembled on the terrace of the manor house, talking, and enjoying the beauty of the star-gemmed sky.

Petrik sat between his mother and Velia.

After a while the talk lulled and silence reigned supreme, save when the slumbering leaves of the motionless trees, waking for a moment, murmured to each other soft whispers, and then slept again.

Presently a meteor, dropping from invisible heights, flashed across the empurpled sky and vanished into space.

Anna Mikailovna, who held Petrik's hand in hers, felt him shudder.

"What was it?" he asked in an agitated voice.

"A falling star, dear."

"Yes, a star," he said pensively. "I knew it was a star."

"You knew it was a star. But how can you know when a star falls, my child?" asked the mother anxiously.

"All the same, he does know," said Velia, joining in the conversation. "There are many things which he knows—one cannot tell how—of himself, intuitively."

This growing sensibility showed that the boy was approaching another critical period of his life, the period between youth and maturity. So far, his intellectual development had been continuous and uneventful. To outward seeming he had, as Maxim desired, become reconciled to his lot, his mental condition being a kind of balanced melancholy, hopeless, perhaps, yet free from acute suffering.

This, however, was merely a respite. Nature makes these short halts, as if for the purpose of affording the young organism time to gather strength for the coming struggle. It is at these periods that new desires and yearnings germinate and ripen beneath the surface. And then, like a bolt from the blue, there comes some sudden shock, and the moral equilibrium is overthrown, and the soul stirred up like the sea by the onset of a storm.

CHAPTER XII.

SEVERAL years glided away.

But the changes at the manor house were few, and to its inmates almost imperceptible. The beech trees still rustled as of yore, only their leaves seemed darker and thicker. The white walls of the mansion still smiled hospitably through the branches; the stable, with its thatched roof, looking only a little more weather-worn, was still visible from the garden, and the strains of Tokim's pipe might be heard nearly every evening at the same time as before. But Tokim, now a middle-aged man and a confirmed bachelor, preferred, when he had the chance, listening to the playing of his young master, whether on the piano or the flute.

Maxim's hair had become quite white; and as

the Popelskys had no other child than Petrik, he was still the principal figure and most important person in the house. For his sake the family held aloof from society, living contentedly their own quiet life, receiving only an occasional visitor and associating almost exclusively with their neighbours at the cottage. Thus Petrik had grown up to manhood like a hot-house plant, shielded from every rough wind and evil influence, knowing nought, save by hearsay, of the troubles, the trials, the triumphs and the pleasures of his fellow-men.

He lived, as always, in the midst of a sightless world. Above and around him stretched illimitable darkness. And Petrik was ever in a condition of keen expectancy. His mind was haunted by a foreboding that this darkness might at any time stretch out to him invisible hands and touch with magnetic fingers something in his soul which was waiting to be wakened out of its long sleep.

Meanwhile, the dull darkness of the manor house

was always filled with soft and caressing voices. The stormy world without might surge and toss, but it was not allowed to ruffle the calm of this monotonous life. In Petrik's imagination it figured as something remote and unreal, like a dream of fairyland or a romance of the unconditioned.

Velia, now a young woman, observed this apathy with her bright steadfast eyes, in which might sometimes be read doubts as to its outcome, but never a sign of impatience. The father, who had greatly improved his estate, thought his son was going on admirably, and neither asked questions nor suggested doubts. Maxim alone regarded his nephew's inertia with impatience and misgiving. On the other hand, it seemed in a measure to fall in with his educational plans. It was a lull, an interlude, which might enable Petrik to gather strength for the battle of life.

But as the years went on and he showed no signs of wakening, the old soldier thought that the time was come for opening wide the windows of the hot-house, and seeing whether a stream of outer air would not rouse Petrik from his dreams.

Maxim began the experiment by asking to the manor his old friend, Stavruchenko, a country gentleman, who lived some fifty miles away. The invitation was readily accepted, and at Maxim's request Stavruchenko brought with him his sons and several other young people who were spending their holidays at his house, and who seized with delight the opportunity of making the old Garibaldian's acquaintance which the visit afforded. He had fought in the sacred cause of freedom, and they honoured him as much as their fathers had feared him.

One of Stavruchenko's sons was an undergraduate at Kief, another a student at the St. Petersburg Conservatory of Music, and they were accompanied by a young military cadet, the son of a neighbouring landowner.

Stavruchenko was a hale, grey-haired, fine old Cossack gentleman. He wore a fancy Cossack dress, sported long Cossack whiskers, and always spoke his native Ruthenian. Though old-fashioned in his ways he was practical in his ideas, and had readily adapted himself to the new conditions created by the emancipation of the serfs. He knew every peasant in his village, could enumerate every cow and almost every piece of money which each of them possessed.

He and his sons—who, following the democratic mode of the period, wore peasants' shirts instead of the European article—bore a striking likeness to Gogol's Taras Bulba and his lads. Though he did not, like Gogol's hero, engage in boxing matches with his sons, he waged with them an incessant wordy warfare. Abroad, as well as at home, the merest trifles were made the pretext for stormy disputes, in which neither party spared the other. The sons had joined those of their generation who went among the people. Their ideas were ultra-democratic. They professed ardent admiration for the peasantry, to whom they ascribed every possible virtue, therein differing so widely from their father that they seldom agreed about anything.

"Only listen to him," he said to Maxim the day after their arrival, when his younger son had been waxing unusually eloquent; "only listen to him! He talks like a book. How clever he is! And yet he let Nicephor take him in."

Whereupon Stavruchenko laughed a great hearty laugh, and the son with much energy protested that the fact of an individual peasant having imposed upon him made no earthly difference, that he studied the people as a whole, and from the only standpoint compatible with broad generalization, whereas practical men, hardened by routine, could not see wood for trees.

"'Hardened by routine' is good. I see you have learned something at college, after all; and yet my man Theodore is more than a match for the pair of you. Come along, Maxim! Ah, here is Popelsky. Shall we go in?"

The three elderly gentlemen now betook themselves to the house, whence loud peals of laughter were presently heard, showing that Stavruchenko was telling one of the humorous stories for which he was famous.

The young people remained in the garden. The student, whom his father had so rudely chaffed, reclined on a peasant's coat, in an attitude of somewhat affected carelessness. His elder brother and the young cadet, whose uniform coat was buttoned up to his chin, sat on the grass near Velia. At some distance, leaning against the window-sill, sat Petrik with bowed head, thinking deeply on the matters mooted in the recent discussion.

"What do you think of all this, Miss Velia?" asked the elder Stavruchenko. "You have not favoured us with your opinion."

"I think all that you said to your father was good. But——"

"But what?"

The girl laid her work on her lap, and smoothed it with her hands, at the same time pensively bending her head. But whether she was examining her embroidery with a view to its improvement, or taking thought about her answer, did not seem quite clear.

The young men waited with expectation. The musical student raised himself on his elbow and looked at Velia; his brother fixed his eyes on her; Petrik, rousing himself, straightened his back and turned his face in the same direction.

"But," said Velia still smoothing her embroidery, "but everybody has to follow his own path in life."

"Heavens, how oracular!" exclaimed the student in a voice expressive of disappointment. "Might I ask, Miss Velia, how old you are?"

"I am eighteen," she answered simply. And then she added with charming *naïveté*, "you tnought I was much older, didn't you?"

The young man laughed.

"Had I been asked your age," replied the elder Stavruchenko, "I should have hesitated whether to say thirteen or three-and-twenty. Really, you know, you sometimes speak like a child, at other times like a wise old woman."

"Serious matters must be seriously dealt with, Gavrilo Petrovitch," answered Velia sententiously, and then went on with her work.

The young men laughed again and then, relapsing into silence, watched Velia curiously as she plied her needle with nimble fingers.

Albeit she was now quite a young woman, Gavrilo Petrovitch's observation as to the difficulty of guessing her age was perfectly correct. As touching her person, she was *petite*, slim, and in figure almost childlike; but her measured and deliberate movements were those of a mature woman. Her features were beautiful and regular; and paradoxical as it may seem, the general expression of her face was at once kindly and cold, mild and firm. Such faces as Velia's are met with only among Sclavonian women. The deep blue eyes were calm, firm and steadfast. Her skin was pearly white; yet not of the whiteness that readily responds to the promptings of passion: rather was it the purer whiteness of unsullied snow.

Velia's fair hair slightly shaded her marble brow, and flowing behind in a heavy tress seemed to draw her head back and give her, as she walked, an upward look.

As for Petrik, although incipient manhood had broadened his body and increased his stature, it had wrought hardly any change in his features. His face was still the same—pale, striking and vividly responsive to his varying moods.

As he sat at some distance from his guests, intently listening to their remarks, his cheeks flushed and paled and flushed again. Now and then the slightly protruding nether lip gave a nervous twitch, while the vague and motionless, albeit large eyes, imparted to the young countenance an abnormally serious and almost gloomy aspect.

"Then we must conclude," said the student, resuming the conversation—"we must conclude that Miss Velia is of opinion that women's minds are inaccessible to such questions as politics and sociology, and that their sphere is the kitchen and the nursery."

There was a mocking note in Gavrilo's voice, and a faint, almost imperceptible blush passed over the girl's fair face.

"You make hasty inductions," she said. "I listened to your conversation, and had no difficulty in understanding it, which shows that at least one woman's mind is accessible to the subjects you mention."

And then she quietly resumed her work.

"Strange!" muttered the young fellow. "It might almost seem that you had marked out your way in life to the very end."

"What would there be strange in that, Gavrilo Petrovitch? Are not people in the habit of choosing their paths in life? Ilia Ivanovitch, the cadet, has chosen his, and he is younger than I am."

"Of course I have," said the cadet, glad of an opportunity of putting in a word. "I have just been reading the biography of General Nementzeff. A fine man he was—a man of rare courage. At twenty he married, and at twenty-five he commanded a regiment and made a good income."

Gavrilo Petrovitch laughed sarcastically; Velia blushed.

"You see, it is as I said," she observed sharply. "Everybody chooses his path in life. What harm if I follow the general example?"

The student made no answer. He, as also the others, felt that the conversation was becoming too personal, and that in Velia's words was a meaning which only herself understood.

CHAPTER XIII.

The discussions which went on almost continually among his guests were for Petrik a revelation; even more, they made an epoch in his life. The generous aspirations of these young people, their bounding hopes, their novel ideas, their talk of the world and its ways stirred his soul to the depths.

At first, he listened with glad surprise; but when he found that in all that went on he had no part, that the high-tide of human interests swept heedlessly past him, his sense of elation changed to a feeling of bitter disappointment. To him alone no question was ever proposed, his the only opinion that was never asked. In these exciting conversations on sociology, politics and what not he felt himself unable to join; he knew so little of them: hence he was as lonely as before, constrained by his infirmity to dwell in a seclusion all the more oppressive as it contrasted so sharply with the new life and animation which his visitors had imparted to the house.

Yet he listened none the less eagerly. The closely-knitted brows and pensive face bespoke increased mental activity, but behind it were bitterness and discontent.

Anna Mikailovna guessed what was passing in

her son's mind, and her heart was heavy with sad forebodings, while Velia's expressive eyes showed that she shared in the mother's uneasiness.

Maxim alone appeared unconcerned, and so well satisfied was he with the result of his experiment that he asked the Stavruchenkos and their friends to come again, a request to which they responded by promising to make another visit at an early date. Petrik accompanied them to the gate, and after a cordial leave-taking, returned slowly towards the house and took a solitary walk in the silent garden.

The silence which in the old days had never troubled him appeared now strange, unusual and ominous of momentous changes in his moral nature and the ideals of his life. With a sudden start he intermitted the hurried pacing to which his deliberate walking had unconsciously increased, and listened intently. It seemed to him as if he could hear among the trees the echo of departed voices; but the next moment he recognized the voices of his mother, his uncle and Velia, who sat at the open windows of the drawing-room, earnestly talking. Though he could not distinguish what they said, it seemed to him that his mother's voice expressed pain and perplexity, that Velia's rang with indignation, and that Maxim was urging unpalatable views with indomitable firmness. Moreover, their talk was evidently about himself, for whenever he approached the window their voices sank into inaudible whisperings.

In truth, Maxim, having deliberately and remorselessly made a breach in the wall which had hitherto hemmed in his pupil from the world, had now to maintain his position against the mother's fears and Velia's doubts.

They saw, as the result of the new departure, that Petrik's ideas were already beginning to overflow the limits of the domestic circle. The quiet of the manor, the lazy rustling of the garden, the monotony of his surroundings, fretted and oppressed him. The darkness had spoken to him with strange voices, and roused with seductive images the inarticulate yearnings which had so long lain dormant in the depths of his soul. Yet not without pain and strivings was this new birth to be accomplished, and the gloom of his countenance showed how sorely he was troubled.

Lady Popelsky and Velia observed these symptoms with doubt and misgiving. Maxim, as they knew, observed them likewise; but he had foreseen them, and regarded them as being in the nature of things. Wherefore the two women, not being philosophers, deemed him hard-hearted and unkind; and Anna Mikailovna, who would have laid down her life for her blind son, asked, with some asperity, what was the good of it all.

A hot-house plant! What mattered that if he were happy? Why should he not remain in the hot-house all the days of his life?

Velia did not venture to speak her thoughts so freely, but her manner, and the sharpness with which she answered Maxim's most innocent remarks, showed that her mind was also ill at ease.

On these occasions the old warrior would look at her from under his thick white brows with keenly inquiring eyes, and hers would give back a glance of anger and defiance.

It might almost seem as if the two were taking stock of each other, as a preliminary to open hostilities.

When the Stavruchenkos returned, a few weeks later, for another visit, Velia received them with cold reserve; yet she could not long withstand the charm of their society, and it would have been discourteous not to bear them company in the walks and excursions in which the days were mostly spent, while the evenings were given to music and conversation.

One evening the talk glided into the delicate and dangerous realm (for Russians) of political discussion. How it happened, or who started the subject nobody could tell. A few common-place phrases, a half-jesting remark from Maxim, and the next moment Gavrilo Petrovitch was making what seemed to Velia almost a set speech. He spoke well and with the youthful enthusiasm which recks nought of danger, and regards the future with either boundless confidence or supreme indifference. In the young man's faith and hopefulness there was something both infectious and fascinating, something which gave to his words the potency of an irresistible summons, a call to duty and self-abnegation.

In this sense Velia understood it, and she felt as if the summons were addressed directly to herself.

She listened eagerly, with head bent low over her work, eyes glistening, cheeks suffused, and wildly beating heart. But the next moment those eyes grew dim, her face paled, and her heart contracted in an agony of fear.

It was as if the great black wall had been rent asunder and she saw through the opening the vast world of toiling, struggling and suffering humanity.

Its grandeur and mystery had attracted her before, but as a dream might, for never before had she realized its actuality and its nearness to herself. Now, it not merely attracted her, it charmed her, asserted rights over her. And yet, and yet—in this world, so strangely revealed to her, there seemed no place for poor blind Petrik.

She raised her eyes and looked at him, and as she looked a sharp pain stung her to the quick. He sat there motionless and buried in thought, his white, drawn face turned towards hers in mute despair.

He understood it all, then. Her thoughts were his thoughts. An icy coldness crept over her, and she felt for a moment as if, without any volition of her own, she had been carried away to the great world of men and women; and looking back she saw Petrik sitting there with his bowed head and sightless eyes, or lying sadly on the hillock by the river, where she had wept over him when they were little children.

The anguish of it was almost more than she could

bear. It was as if somebody were trying to withdraw the knife from her old wound and had made it bleed afresh.

Now she understood the meaning of Maxim's scrutinizing glances. He knew her better than she knew herself. He saw that her mind was unsettled and had doubts as to the choice she might eventually make. But now. . . . Now, she was resolved as to what she should do, do without delay—at once. Afterwards she would see her way more clearly.

Velia drew a deep breath as if she had been engaged in violent physical exercise. The speaker's voice was hushed; but how long he had spoken, or when stopped speaking she had no idea. She looked round for Petrik. Petrik was not there.

The girl rolled up her embroidery and rose from her seat.

"Pray excuse me. I will be back presently," she said to the guests, who being again deep in discussion neither heard her apology nor, for some time afterwards, observed her absence.

Turning into the garden, she walked softly along an avenue, darkened by overarching trees, a favourite resort of Petrik's. She had not gone far when, at a bend in the path, she heard the voices of Maxim and Lady Popelsky in earnest, almost impassioned, conversation.

"You may be sure that I thought of her as much as of him," the old man was saying sternly. "Think of it! She is little more than a child, and knows nothing of life. I cannot believe that you would take advantage of her ignorance."

"But—if—if she—— What will become of my poor boy?" asked Anna Mikailovna piteously.

"That we must leave. We shall see, and it may be—— But worse than anything else would be to lay on his conscience the ruin of another's life. And upon ours also. Think of it, dear Anna—think of it. This must not be." As Maxim spoke he raised his sister's hand to his lips, and her agitation was so great that she could scarce hold herself erect.

"My poor, poor boy!"

Velia guessed rather than heard these words, which came like a cry from the mother's heart.

A wave of warm blood rushed to the girl's face, and she stopped dubiously at the turning of the path. If she went further Maxim and Lady Popelsky would see that they had been overheard.

After a moment's hesitation she raised her head proudly. What had she to fear? The overhearing was an accident. To retreat furtively would look like conscious guilt, as if she had been playing the eavesdropper. Moreover, the old man took too much on himself. She was quite capable of choosing her own path in life.

So with head erect Velia turned the corner of the avenue, and walked quickly past the rustic bench where the brother and sister were sitting. Maxim involuntarily drew back his crutches to let her pass; and Anna Mikailovna followed her with eyes that spoke a love more than motherly, a love so chastened and yet so impassioned that it bordered on reverence and fear, for she knew that on this proud girl, who had just gone so haughtily by, depended the happiness or the misery of her dear boy's life.

CHAPTER XIV.

AT the bottom of the garden were the ruins of an old mill. For long years the big wheel had been idle and was fast falling into decay; the shafts were moss grown; the clear water, oozing through the old sluices, fell in tiny cascades, filling the air with silvery music. Here was Petrik's favourite retreat. He would sit for hours on the edge of the dyke, musing pleasantly as he listened to the waterfall's voice and the nightingale's song, both of which he could reproduce with wonderful fidelity on the flute or the piano. But now he has other thoughts; his soul is troubled within him, his heart full of bitterness, his face drawn with pain.

After sitting for a few minutes on the grassy slope he rises with a gesture of impatience, and paces rapidly to and fro in the shadow of the trees. He is too ill at ease to remain still, and so absorbing are his thoughts that he hears not the light footstep he knows so well, and starts violently when Velia's hand is laid lightly on his shoulder.

"What is the matter with you, Petrik? Why are you so sad?" she asks in her low, sweet voice.

He turned aside without answering and resumed his walk. Velia said no more, but walked on by his side, for she guessed his thoughts and knew that this rudeness was not rudely meant. Just then somebody in the house began to sing. A young, powerful voice, softened by distance, sang of love and happiness, and, spreading far and wide in the quiet of the summer night, drowned alike the rustling of the trees and the music of the mill stream.

Only a moment ago she was with them, the fortunate ones, who talked of the busy world and the bright full life without, and whose dreams were of a future in which he could have no part.

And he—how long had he been there in darkness and grief?

They walked on in silence. Never before had Velia found it so difficult to soothe and console him. But she knew that her company always calmed him and chased away his gloom; and after a while she noticed with gladness that his brow cleared and his pace slackened. The charm of her presence was beginning to tell. Gradually his mental anguish passed away and gave place to another feeling—not for the first time—a feeling which he could not define, but whose wholesome influence he willingly acknowledged.

"What is the matter, Petrik?" asked Velia again.

"Nothing particular," he answered bitterly. "I was only thinking that for me this world, of which they talk so much, has no place."

For a while the singing had ceased, but now it recommenced, though Velia and Petrik being at some distance from the house it was only faintly heard. Gavrilo was singing an old ballad, the air of which resembled the hum of the Ruthenian bandor. At times it seemed to die away; then after a moment of suspense and expectation the soft melody would rise again and float over the garden and through the trees, bringing with it the perfume of flowers.

Petrik stopped to listen.

"Do you know," he said sadly, "I sometimes think old people are right when they say the world is worse than it used to be in their young days. In old times it was better for the blind. If I had been living then I should have had a bandor and been a wandering minstrel. People would have crowded round me, and I should have sung to them the deeds of their forefathers, of love, and glory and war. I should have been somebody, whilst now—— Even this cadet, whose sole ambition is to marry and make a good income, —you remember what he said. They laughed at him; but I am not even equal to that."

The girl's blue eyes were troubled, and an unbidden tear trickled slowly down her cheek.

"You have allowed yourself to be too much affected by Gavrilo Petrovitch's eloquence," she said with ill-assumed indifference, for she also had been more touched by the same eloquence than she cared to own—even to herself.

"Yes," answered Petrik dreamily. "What a fine fellow he is! And he has such a good voice."

"Yes, I think he is a good man," returned the girl pensively, almost tenderly indeed, as if it pleased her to echo Petrik's praises of the eloquent student.

But the next moment, as if she had suddenly bethought her of something which it behoved her not to forget, she exclaimed sharply, "No, I do not like him a bit. He is too self-complacent by half, and his voice is harsh and dissonant. I don't like him, I tell you."

Petrik listened to this strange outbreak in mute

surprise. Only a minute ago she was praising Gavrilo, and now——

Velia with an angry stamp of her foot, went on: "It is all a farce; I understand perfectly. Maxim has got it all up for a purpose. I hate him."

"Hate Uncle Maxim! Why, Velia, what has he done to offend you?"

"To offend me? It is not so much me. But don't you see? He considers himself very clever, and thinks that others are as heartless as himself. Oh, I understand. Don't mention him! And what right has he to take upon himself the disposal of other people's destinies?"

She stopped abruptly, wrung her hands, and burst into tears. This outburst on the part of one so calm and self-possessed as Velia surprised Petrik greatly, and her weeping so moved him with strange, unutterable feelings that he knew not what to say or how to console her. He could only take both her hands in his and wait until she spoke again.

For a moment Velia remained silent, as if she were struggling with unspeakable thoughts. Then, abruptly freeing her hands, she fell a-laughing.

Petrik was now completely bewildered, and finding himself in the presence of a mystery, wisely held his tongue and waited for developments.

"How stupid I am! Why do I cry?" said Velia, recovering her self-possession and wiping away her tears. "No, let us be just. These young men are brave and good. And Gavrilo Petrovitch's sentiments are good and true."

"For all who can live up to them," observed Petrik gloomily.

"And if there be some who cannot, what then? People can only make the most of such opportunities as they have. Maxim had to give up soldiering when he lost his leg and fingers. All the same, he finds a place in the world. So shall we."

"Don't say 'we.' You may; but for me it is out of the question."

"Not at all."

"How can you say so?"

"Because—well, because you will marry me, and our lives will be the same."

Petrik stopped again, more astounded than ever, but this time he found words.

"I marry you!" he gasped. "Then you will be my wife?"

"Yes, yes, of course," she answered in an agitated voice, in which there was a shade of impatience. "Dear me! How stupid you are! Is it possible you never thought of it? It is so natural. Whom else could you marry?"

"Whom else? You are right," he said complacently and with a serene smile. And then another thought occurred to him and his face saddened again. "Listen, Velia, dear," he added, taking her hand. "You have just heard how girls live in society; how they amuse themselves; how they go about and learn everything. The wide world is before you, but I——"

"Well, what about you?"

"I am blind."

"So you are. But what then?" said Velia, smiling in her turn. "If a girl falls in love with a blind man she must marry him, though he is blind. It is a thing that cannot be helped."

Petrik smiled again, and dreamily bent his head, as if the thoughts which surged up from the inmost recesses of his being were too big for words. The lovers kept silence, listening to the voices of the night—the petals of the cherry blossoms falling softly at their feet, the music of the mill stream and the sweet piping of the nightingale and the rustle of the trees in the grove behind the old mill.

By the bold and resolute, yet, considering the circumstances, not unmaidenly step she had taken, Velia had reconciled Petrik to his affliction and chased away the cloud which was troubling his peace. The deep feeling which had struck its roots into his heart, he could not tell when, had developed and strengthened with time, and now that he understood its significance pervaded his whole being. Why had he not understood it sooner?

For a while he stood motionless; then, raising his head, he threw back his hair and pressed tenderly the little hand which he held in his. He was surprised to find how strangely the answering pressure affected him. Formerly they shook hands almost automatically. Now the slight movement of her small fingers sent a responsive thrill to his heart, filling it with a strange happiness. Velia, his childhood's friend, had all at once become a woman whom he loved and who loved him.

When he remembered her tears, so lately shed, it seemed to him that he was strong and powerful, she tender and weak. He would be her protector, and cherish her and minister to her all his life long. He drew her lovingly to his breast and toyed with her silky hair. His happiness was complete. No more vague yearnings, no more unappeasable desires. He forgot even his blindness, feeling for the moment as if neither heaven nor earth had aught more to give him.

They were roused from their abstraction by the nightingale, which, after singing several airs, gave one long impassioned trill and then abruptly stopped.

"Enough, dearest; let me go!" said Velia, freeing herself from her lover's embrace.

Petrik, having just then no other idea than to do Velia's bidding, made no attempt to detain her.

"As you like, darling. You are putting up your hair."

"How do you know?"

"I can hear."

"You hear everything. I sometimes think that you know better what is going on than those who can see."

"You have done putting up your hair. Give me your hand."

"No; we must go and rejoin the guests. We have been out quite long enough. Come!"

And with that she led the way towards the house, Petrik submissively following, his heart full to overflowing, yet beating pleasantly and strongly withal, and giving him a joyous sense of energy and hopefulness such as he had never before known or imagined.

CHAPTER XV.

The guests, host and hostess and Maxim were by this time in the drawing-room. Only Petrik and Velia were wanting. Maxim was in close converse with his old comrade. The others sat in silence at the open windows, all being more or less under the sway of the peculiar nervous tension that affects people when they know, or divine, that a domestic drama is going on of which they are supposed to be ignorant, or of which policy or politeness compels them to pretend ignorance.

Though Maxim made as if he listened with great attention to his friend's observations and anecdotes, he never took his eyes off the door. Anna Mikailovna tried to look cheerful and unconcerned, but her countenance showed that her mind was ill at ease. Mr. Popelsky, fast asleep in his chair, was alone insensible to the dominant influence of the hour.

When the sound of footsteps was heard on the terrace leading from the drawing-room, all eyes were turned in that direction, and presently Velia's sylph-like figure was framed, as it were, in the wide doorway.

To her followed Petrik.

After a moment's pause the girl entered the room, showing neither concern nor self-consciousness, albeit every eye was curiously scanning her countenance. Maxim's inquiring glance was met with a smile half merry, half defiant, which so disconcerted him that for the first time in his life he answered at random, to the great surprise of Stavruchenko, who mentally noted that the old soldier was not the man he used to be.

Meanwhile, Anna Mikailovna was intently watching her son.

Petrik followed Velia absently, as if he did not realize whither she was leading him. At the threshold he stopped for an instant, just as Velia had done; and then, still absently, and with a strangely rapt look on his sightless face, made straight for the piano. It seemed as if, forgetting where he was and that he was not alone, he had no other thought than to express, through his favourite instrument, the feelings which possessed his soul.

Opening the piano, he sat down and swept his hands over the keyboard with a light, rapid touch. He appeared to be asking something, either of the piano or of his own mind.

Then, with his fingers resting on the keys, he sank into silent meditation. Every voice in the room was hushed. The brooding night looked in through the windows; the birch trees, made visible by the light of the lamps, swayed gently to the dying wind. The guests, roused to keen attention by the preliminary murmur of the piano and the inspired look of the blind musician, sat in mute suspense.

Still Petrik remained silent and motionless, his head uplifted as if he were communing with an invisible spirit. Unutterable thoughts were surging in his soul, like the waves of a wind-swept sea. The current of a new life had seized him, as the tide seizes and carries away a stranded boat. He sought for something which, as yet, he could neither define or understand. His eyes opened widely, then contracted and filled with tears.

For a while it seemed as if he failed to find in his soul that which he so ardently desired, but at length, with a great effort, he broke the spell; his fingers moved again, and soon a series of wonderful melodies, now soft and plaintive, now passionate and melting, broke the silence of the night.

These were the musical rendering of harmonies which his sensitive memory had been gathering up during nearly the whole of his conscious life; the wail of the wind, the rustling of the forest, the plash of the rain, the howling of the storm, the sound of human voices dying out in the distance, the rhythmical expression of the otherwise inarticulate feelings which communion with nature kindles in a responsive soul. The first notes struck by the improvisatore were dubious and hesitating, as if his imagination were struggling with a flood of chaotic memories, against which he found it impossible to make head.

Then the air became more definite and concrete; only a few bold touches were required to convert it into a noble melody. The listeners held their breath, and Maxim wondered where his nephew could have found so great a wealth of impressions. But before it had reached its full height the flood of melody subsided into a piteous moan—as a wave that wastes itself in spray and foam—and ended in a note of bitter perplexity and doubt.

The music stopped. The charm which had held

the listeners spell-bound was broken; the lamps seemed to burn more dimly, the brooding night to look through the dark windows more sternly than before.

But ere the guests could voice their thoughts, the musician, gathering confidence from doubt and boldness from perplexity, struck the keys once more; and once more the melody grew in fulness and strength, rising ever higher, as if towards some lofty and unattainable ideal.

Then another change. Without pause or let, Petrik glided into one of the charming Ruthenian melodies which were associated with his earliest memories. It breathed now love, now sadness, now the bright hopefulness of youth, now a tale of glory and war, heroism and suffering. Instead of improvising he was trying to express his varying moods in the popular airs of his native land.

But it ended in a strain of tremulous melancholy, as if some insoluble question were still troubling his mind.

For his third essay Petrik chose a piece of music which he had learnt from notes, in the hope, it may be, of bringing his feelings into harmony with those of the composer.

Now, the blind have great difficulty in learning from notes. Every piece which they acquire in this way must be played by rote, and much dry work is required before the arbitrary detached signs by which each note is indicated can be transformed into a complete melody. Petrik loved music so ardently that he had studied it closely and methodically. But his rich musical imagination made it hard for him, when playing a set piece, to adhere strictly to the text. To everything which he played Petrik gave the stamp of his own genius, attuning it to the ideals he had formed and the Nature with which he had so closely communed all his life long.

And now, as he played with beating heart and glowing face the piece which he had selected, his hearers listened with unconcealed admiration and glad surprise. Soon, however, they were again carried away by the artist's brilliant originality, and forgot everything but his playing and himself. Only the elder of the brothers, a professional musician and musical critic, kept an unmoved countenance and tried to analyze the peculiarities of Petrik's style.

True music is outside the strife of opinions and the conflicts of cliques. The eyes of the young people glistened, and their faces flushed with the bold and generous thoughts which the blind musician had kindled in their hearts. Even the matter-of-fact and sceptical Stavruchenko was unable to withstand the wizard's power. For a while he listened silently and with bowed head. But as the music went on his face became more and more animated. Touching Maxim on the shoulder, he said in an intense whisper:

"That is what I call playing. Yes, that is indeed playing."

Velia sat with folded hands, regarding her lover with tender admiration. She understood his melodies in a way peculiar to herself, hearing in them the sweet purling of the stream by the old mill, and the soft fall of cherry blossoms in a darkened avenue.

But, strangely enough, the blind musician's face gave no indication that he shared in, or even felt, the enthusiasm with which he had inspired his hearers. It seemed as if his heart-searchings had, as yet, found no answer to the questions which troubled his peace. Only his mother, who was watching him with painful solicitude, recognized a something in his look and in his gestures that reminded her of the spring day long ago, when her boy, overwhelmed by a flood of new sensations, fell senseless on the mound by the river. But it came and went like the shadow of a passing cloud; and the next moment there arose a hum of voices. Everybody was talking at once, and old Stavruchenko, still under the spell of the music, folded Petrik in his fatherly arms as if the young man had been a small boy.

"You play gloriously, my dear lad," he exclaimed excitedly.

The young people, equally excited, took him by the hand, and the student predicted for him a brilliant artistic future.

"Yes," said his brother thoughtfully, "you are quite right. I also think he will have a brilliant future. You have caught in a wonderful way the spirit of our national melodies. But what was that air you played last?"

Petrik named a piece by a well-known Italian *maestro*.

"I thought so. Yes, I know the piece. But you have a very original style. Many play it better than you; but nobody plays it as you play it."

"Why then do you say that others play it better?" asked Stavruchenko.

"Well, you see, I have generally heard it played faithfully, after the original. But Petrik's version seems to be a translation from the Italian into our native Ruthenian music."

Petrik listened attentively. It was the first time in his life that he had been made so much of, or heard his playing discussed as a matter of general interest, and a proud consciousness of power thrilled his heart. He had a place in the world, after all.

He was sitting pensively on the music stool, with his back to the piano and one hand resting on the music-stand, when he felt a warm touch on his fingers. It was Velia, who, taking his hand in hers, whispered joyfully in his ear:

"You hear what they say! It is as I told you. There is a place in the world for you to fill. Who knows what, with your genius for music, you may not be able to achieve?"

Petrik raised his head proudly, his face radiant with hope. Only his mother observed this episode. Her face also beamed with pleasure, beamed as brightly as the face of a young girl who receives the first kiss of passionate love.

Velia moved away, but Petrik remained where

he was, and in the same attitude as before. His face grew pale again, paler than usual. He was struggling with the overwhelming emotions of the great happiness which had come to him. It may be, also, that he had a foreboding of the storm which, rising from some dark recess of his brain, threatened for a time the shipwreck of his hopes and the ruin of his life.

CHAPTER XVI.

On the next morning Petrik woke up early. All was quiet, both in the room and in the house. The fragance of the new-born day flowed in through the open windows. But, as yet, he was still so much under the influence of the drowsy god that his memory had not reproduced, in their fulness the incidents of the previous evening. Nevertheless, a sense of satisfaction and delight, such as he had never known before, pervaded his being.

For a few minutes he lay listening to the

feathered songsters of the grove, who just then broke into a joyous carol. This roused him to full consciousness.

"What has befallen me?" he asked himself. And as if in answer to the question there came back to him Velia's exclamation:

"Never thought of it before! Dear me, how stupid you are!"

It was quite true. He had not thought of it before. Almost as long as he could remember her presence had been the greatest pleasure of his life; yet until yesterday he had no more consciously felt it than he felt the life-giving oxygen in the air which he breathed.

He woke up a new man, and she, his old companion, appeared to him as if transfigured. Recalling and dwelling delightedly on all that had happened the day before, he heard again, in imagination, the witching melody of her low sweet voice, as it spoke of their love and revealed the secret of their hearts.

Hastily rising, he dressed quickly and ran down to the old mill. The water murmured, the trees rustled and the blossoms fell as they had done yesterday, in the gloaming. But then it was dark, and now it was full daylight. Never before had Petrik felt the daylight so vividly. It seemed as if the sweet moist air of the morning and the bright rays of the rising sun were entering his very body and sending through its nervous system a stream of new and delightful sensations.

But soon this sense of delight was followed by something very different—at first, however, so indefinite that he hardly noticed it. Gathering in some unknown depth of his consciousness, it grew and expanded like a small cloud—at the beginning no bigger than a man's hand—which appearing on the verge of the azure sky spreads until it darkens the whole horizon.

Only a few minutes ago he heard her voice whispering in his ear; he toyed with her silky hair; pressed her responsive hand and held her in his arms. It seemed so real that his heart throbbed with a joy too great for words.

Now all was gone, gone as utterly as the formless phantoms of the night. In vain he paced to and fro in the avenue, in vain threw himself down on the mill stream bank, and tried to conjure back the beloved apparition. He could recall every word she had spoken, every tone of her voice, every movement she had made. But he could no longer materialize them into the harmonious enchanting personality which he knew as Velia. And soon her voice itself vanished like the voice of a dream; even the sense of his new happiness became deadened; then faded utterly away, leaving behind an aching void, followed by a wild passionate yearning for that which might never be.

He wanted to see her.

The love which had made him a new man and given him so many exquisite sensations had also awakened in him a fatal something which was a source of intense suffering.

He loved Velia, and he wanted to see her.

CHAPTER XVII.

AFTER the departure of the guests life at the manor house resumed its wonted calm. But a great change had been wrought in Petrik's character. He grew nervous and irritable, his moods changeable and capricious. There were times when Velia's presence would charm away the evil spirit and make him as happy and lively as of yore. But after a while these brighter intervals became shorter and less frequent. Velia's influence perceptibly waned, and moments of passionate tenderness alternated with days of settled gloom.

At length, Anna Mikailovna's worst fears were realized. She discovered that dreams, like those which had troubled her son's childhood, were again making his nights hideous.

Early one morning she stole into Petrik's bedroom. He slept; but not the wholesome sleep of a healthy body and a tranquil soul. He tossed about on his pillow; his face was pale and troubled, and the half-opened sightless eyes stared stolidly from under their long dark lashes.

The mother watched him with keen anxiety, trying to think what could be the cause of his agitation, which visibly increased as she looked on.

And then a strange thing happened; a thing which, to her excited imagination, appeared weird, uncanny and almost supernatural.

Something—a hardly perceptible gleam—glided rapidly over the bed. Then a ray of yellow sunlight fell on the wall above Petrik's pillows and glided slowly downward, until it reached the half-open eyes of the sleeper, the pallor of whose face had meanwhile increased almost to ghastliness. Next, the ray, which might have been alive, mingled with Petrik's hair and settled on his forehead. The mother bent forward, as if to shield him from the malign influence of the impish sunbeam; but her feet refused to move, and now she stood as if spell-bound. The sleeper's eyelids opened wide, the motionless pupils emitted sparks; his head visibly uplifted, as if raised from the pillow by the flood of light which now shone into the room. Something between a smile and a sigh contorted his features, and then his face became as pallid as before—the image of desperate effort.

Here Anna Mikailovna broke the spell which had chained her limbs, and going to the bedside she laid her hand on Petrik's head. He awoke with a start.

"You, mother?" he asked in surprise.

"Yes, dear, it is I."

He raised himself on his elbow, and looked as if he were trying to collect his thoughts or recall some fleeting memory. And then, with a gesture of disappointment, he said:

"I have seen things in a dream again. I often

see things now. But no, I cannot (sighing)—I can recall nothing."

A year passed, and there was still no improvement in Petrik's condition. His melancholy seemed to have become chronic, showing itself chiefly in an excessive nervous irritability, which went hand in hand with a morbid increase of sensitiveness. His ear acquired a wonderful subtlety. He felt light with his whole organism. He could even distinguish moonlight from moonless nights. Often, when all in the house were asleep, he would get up and, going into the garden, sit there, sad and motionless, a prey to the dreamy and mysterious influence of the queen of the night, whose silvery rays, as she moved through the purple sky, shone on his face and were reflected in his eyes. When she approached the horizon and shrouded herself in a crimson mist, Petrik's countenance would soften and he would return to his room in a less despondent frame of mind.

What he thought about during these long vigils

it were hard to say. To every one who has known the joys and sorrows of intellectual existence there comes a time when he must pass through a spiritual crisis. Standing on the verge of active life the individual man tries to determine his position in the world, his relations to his fellow-men and the purpose and aim of that life. Few are those who can undergo this ordeal without mental suffering. For Petrik the crisis was unusually trying. To the question: "What has a man to live for?" he had to add: "What has a blind man to live for?" In Petrik's case, moreover, this mental travail was intensified by the almost physical pressure of an unsatisfied need. He secluded himself more and more; his moods were at times so uncertain that even Velia feared to speak to him, lest she might thereby aggravate his wretchedness, instead of appeasing his melancholy.

"You think I love you?" he asked her one day sharply.

"I know you do, dear."

"And I don't," he said in a tone of deep dejection. "No, I don't know. There was a time when I thought my love for you was greater than all the world. But now I doubt it. I don't know myself. Leave me. Follow those who call you to another life before it is too late."

"Oh, why will you torment me so?" she demanded reproachfully.

"I torment you!" exclaimed Petrik in a tone which bespoke both egotism and suffering. "I torment you! Well, so I do. And I shall go on tormenting you in the same way all my life; I cannot help it. You know I must. Go away. Leave me to my fate. I can repay your love only with misery."

"I want to see," he would say when in a more reasonable mood. "I want to see; and do what I will, I cannot get rid of the want. It is always with me. If I could see but once, were it only in a dream—see the sky, and the earth, and the bright, beautiful sun, and then remember them for ever; if I could see my father and mother, Maxim and yourself, I should be content, and suffer no more all my life long."

And his mind dwelt always on this one idea. Another day Petrik and Velia were in the drawing-room, when Maxim came in. The girl looked unhappy and perplexed, and Petrik's face wore the expression of brooding melancholy and bitter discontent which of late had become almost habitual to it. To find out fresh doubts and difficulties and torment himself and perplex others therewith, had become a sort of necessity for him.

"He has been asking me," said Velia to Maxim, "what people mean by saying that melodies have colours, and I cannot tell him."

"What does it matter?" said the old man curtly.

Petrik shrugged his shoulders.

"Nothing particular. Only I thought that if sounds have colours—and I cannot see colours—it follows that even sounds are not fully accessible to me."

"Nonsense! You know that it is not so—that sounds are more accessible to you than to any of us."

"But what does the expression mean, then? It surely has a meaning."

"It is a metaphor, a means of comparison, nothing more; and as sound and light are really in their essence vibrations, there must needs be a certain analogy between them."

"But what properties are implied in the idea of a melody or a tune having colour?" insisted Petrik obstinately.

Maxim thought for a moment.

"Don't you remember that when you were a child your mother tried to make you understand the differences in colour by sounds?"

"Yes, and you stopped us. Why? If we had gone on I should perhaps have understood."

"I don't think you would. Nevertheless, I think

that in certain states of human consciousness the impressions produced by light and sound must be nearly identical. When we say of any one that he sees things in a rosy light, we mean that he is in a joyful mood. Now the same mood may be produced by a combination of sounds, and as a rule the colours and the sounds are symbols of the same emotions."

Maxim lighted his pipe and studied his nephew's face. Petrik sat in an attitude of attention, as if he wanted to hear more.

"Shall I go on?" his uncle asked himself; and then, after a preliminary pull at his pipe, he continued:

"Red is the emblem of joy and passion."

"Red—warm?" said Petrik interrogatively.

"Yes, red and warm. Fruit is always redder on the side which is exposed to the warm rays of the sun. It is thus that the bloom and intensity of life, the passion of vegetable nature seem to be concentrated. You see that even in the inanimate world red is the colour of passion. It is also the colour of joy, sin, anger, fury, and the emblem of implacable revenge. But do you understand all this?"

"Never mind, go on."

Maxim puffed vigorously at his pipe until his head was half hidden in the resulting smoke, and then proceeded:

"It is the same with other colours. For instance, the sky is blue; wherefore we associate blue with the idea of unruffled serenity. When the sky is deep blue it gives us a sense of calmness and security. But when it is hidden from us by sombre, storm-laden clouds, we feel troubled and oppressed. You feel the approach of a storm yourself?"

"Yes, I feel apprehensive and uneasy."

"Exactly. We are all anxious for the sky to reappear; it does us good. The sky is blue; the sea also, when it is calm. Your mother's eyes are blue, so are Velia's."

"Like the sky?" said Petrik tenderly.

"Yes, and blue eyes are held to betoken serenity of soul. Green is the prevailing colour of nature. It suggests quiet enjoyment and good health, but not passion, or what men call happiness .... Do you understand?"

"Not quite ... but never mind. Go on, please."

"In this part of the world there comes every year a time when visible life dies on the earth's surface, and snow falls on it and it becomes white and smooth. White is the colour of the cold snow, and of the clouds that float at immeasurable heights above the earth, of grand and sterile mountain peaks, like the Alps and the Himalayas. It is the emblem of impassibility, of cold high sanctity, and of future incorporeal life. As for black——"

"I know," interrupted Petrik. "It is—when there is no sound, no movement—night."

"Yes, and that is why black is the emblem of death."

"Ah, death! death!" said the young fellow gloomily. "You speak of blackness and death. Well, for me the world is all blackness. Death! Death! Everywhere and always."

"No, Petrik; emphatically, no," answered Maxim warmly. "Sound, music, warmth, language, all these are accessible to you."

"It is true," said Petrik dreamily. "Yes, I know, if you like, the warm red sounds, the tender blue sounds, and the proud white ones, which soar at unreachable heights. But those nearest to me are the dark sounds of sorrow and suffering, which spread low over the face of the earth. You know that now, when I play, I feel no joy, rather as if I could weep."

"Listen, Petrik," said the old man seriously, rising from his seat. "In yearning after the unattainable, you forget the blessings which you already possess. Think how tenderly you are cared for, how lovingly you have been watched, and helped and taught, from your cradle to this very day. But you do not see this; and you suffer and repine simply because you are eaten up with egotism. You are so much absorbed by the thought of your affliction that you have no room in your mind for aught else."

"You are right," returned Petrik warmly. "It does absorb me, and I cannot get away from it. It is always with me, follows me everywhere."

"Ah, Petrik! If you only knew, if you could only realize that there are people in the world whose afflictions are a hundred times greater than yours, whose lives are so wretched that compared with it your life, surrounded by kindness, comfort and love, is a very heaven of happiness, then——"

"It is not true—it is not true," interrupted the young man passionately. "I would willingly exchange my lot for that of the veriest beggar— for the veriest beggar is more fortunate than I am. It is wrong to make so much of the blind, to surround them with comforts and luxuries. Far better turn them adrift and let them shift for themselves. If I were a common beggar I should be a happier man. I should have something to do, my thoughts would always be occupied. In the morning I should have to think how to get my dinner, or how to lay out my coppers to the best advantage. When I made a good haul I should be in high spirits, and sure of a supper and a night's lodgings. And if things went ill with me, and I had to endure hunger and cold, I should at least have food for thought, and my time would be well filled. At the worst, I should not suffer so much as I suffer now."

"Are you sure of that?" asked Maxim coldly; but as he looked towards Velia his eyes spoke kindness and compassion. She looked pale, anxious and perplexed.

"Quite sure," answered Petrik abruptly, almost rudely indeed.

"I don't care to argue the point with you," said Maxim in the same tone of cold indifference. "Perhaps you are right, and, in any case, though your life might be harder, you would be a better man. At present you talk and act like a sheer egotist."

And with that the old soldier, after another pitying glance at Velia, clattered out of the room in a cloud of smoke.

This conversation left Petrik pretty much as it found him. At any rate, it neither cured him of his egotism nor reconciled him to his lot. Rather, by exciting him to fresh efforts, did it aggravate his discontent. There were times when he almost succeeded in realizing the sensations which his uncle had described.

The dark sad earth receded far far away from him, and over all stretched a vast canopy. He heard the dread din of heaven's artillery, and faintly realized the awful infinity of space. Then the thunder ceased, stillness reigned, and his soul was at peace. Sometimes with these visions were mingled the voices of Velia and his mother.

But these mental struggles and vague conceptions tormented his soul without satisfying his aspirations. They entailed strenuous effort, and were yet so powerless that their sole effect was to sharpen the pain of a sick soul, striving in vain to reach the fulness of its impressions.

CHAPTER XVIII.

SOME forty miles from the manor was a small country town, which had the good fortune to possess a miraculous Catholic ikon. The character and extent of the ikon's wonder-working powers were determined with perfect accuracy by those learned in such matters. All who went afoot to pay homage to the ikon on its name-day were granted twenty days' indulgence, which meant that by so much would the sojourn of their souls in purgatory be shortened.

This time fell in the autumn, and coincided with the annual fair, and so many pilgrims and beggars, buyers and sellers, streamed into the town, and it became so altered, that it hardly knew itself.

The old church was decked inside and out with garlands and green boughs. Its bells rang merry peals all day long. The carriages of the neighbouring gentry rattled and rumbled over the pavement in endless procession. The pilgrims thronged the streets and squares, and many, unable to find quarters in the town, encamped in the fields.

On the great day the church was beset with people of all sorts, ages and conditions, and the roads leading thither were lined with beggars holding out their hands for alms.

To any one looking down on the spectacle from above it would have seemed like a gigantic serpent, now lying motionless, now shaking its many-coloured scales, and moving slowly forward.

The footpaths on either side of the street were lined with beggars asking for alms. Among the people in the street were Maxim, Petrik and

Tokim. They had come to the fair, and, having completed their purchases, were wending back, as fast as the press would let them, to their inn. Suddenly Maxim's dark eyes brightened, and with the air of a man struck by a happy thought he turned into a lane leading towards the fields.

As they went on the shouts of the loud-throated crowd, the cries of the Jewish pedlars and the rattle of vehicles lost their individuality, and merged into a sound like the roar of a distant sea.

Outside the town the crowd was thinner, yet even here there was a confused din of footsteps, wheels and human voices.

To these discordant noises Petrik listened absently, his mind full of confused and discordant thoughts. Every now and then, as he followed his uncle, wondering whither he was leading him, the young fellow would shiver and draw his overcoat closer round him, for the day was bitterly cold.

But he was suddenly roused from his reverie

by something which affected him so painfully that he trembled from head to foot and stopped abruptly.

They were in the open country, at a spot where many years before some pious soul had built a stone pillar, with an ikon and a lantern whose sole purpose, as it might seem, was to creak dismally in the wind, for it was never lighted.

At the foot of this pillar sat a group of blind beggars, driven thither by their sighted companions, who had taken possession of all the better places. Each of them held out a wooden bowl, and every now and then one of them would intone a pitiful appeal to the passers-by.

"Give to the blind ones
Give to the blind ones,
For Christ His sake."

Here the beggars had been sitting from early morning, exposed to the full blast of the piercing wind which blew from the steppe. They could not, like others, go into the town and move about to warm themselves, and the piteous refrain, which every one struck up in turn, was a wail of acute misery and physical pain. The first notes were high-pitched, and then, as if the singer were too weak and wretched to continue, they melted into a doleful murmur, ending in a heart-breaking sigh and an audible shiver of cold.

Petrik stood spell-bound, his face expressing as much horror as if his sight had been restored and he saw before him a Gorgon's head or a "goblin damned."

"Why do you look so frightened?" asked Maxim quietly. "These are the happy blind beggars, whose lot you were so much envying the other day. They are holding out their hands for alms. It is in this way they get their living. They feel a little cold, I dare say, for even you and I shiver a little, though we are warmly clad and well fed; but their clothes are in tatters, and they look ravenously hungry; that, however, is good for them—gives them something to think about and look forward to, you know, and makes them beg with all the more energy."

"Let us go away at once, please. Let us go, let us go!" exclaimed Petrik, taking his uncle's hand.

"What? You want to be off already? Is this the only idea suggested to you by their sufferings? You might at least throw the poor wretches a copper, like everybody else. Only the other day you were making light of the sufferings of unfortunates such as these, and now you actually want to run away, because their appeals give you a sense of discomfort."

It was a bitter lesson, and Petrik bowed his head in humiliation and shame; but he took out his purse and went to the beggar who was just then wailing his doleful ditty. Groping first with his stick and next with his hand he found the wooden bowl, and emptied into it the contents of his purse.

Several passers-by stopped and regarded with surprise the well-dressed good-looking gentleman who was groping with a stick, feeling with his hands, and giving alms to beggars as blind as himself.

Maxim watched Petrik keenly, and Tokim, wiping away the tear which trickled down his cheek, said reproachfully:

"It is a shame. Oh, sir, you should not try him so hard."

In the meantime Petrik, having received the beggar's blessing, returned to his uncle, his face pale and dejected, his manner humble and subdued.

"May I go now?" he murmured, "for God's sake!"

Maxim turned round and walked briskly towards the town. His nephew's strange looks alarmed him, and he asked himself whether he had not, as Tokim said, made the ordeal too severe.

Petrik followed him silently, battling with bowed head against the icy blast which was blowing in their faces clouds of dust.

The next morning he was laid up with a violent fever, and before night became delirious. His usually pale face was suffused with blood, and he tossed about on his pillow, muttering, and appearing to listen to something which only he could hear. Sometimes he tried to leap from his bed and run away, and had to be held down by main force.

The old surgeon who had been called in, after feeling his patient's pulse and observing his face, said something about the wind.

Maxim knitted his brows and shook his head. He did not think the wind had much to do with it.

The illness proved to be serious, and after the delirium had spent its force Petrik lay several days almost as still as if he were bereft of life.

In the end, however, his youthful constitution and careful nursing pulled him through.

One bright autumn morning, nearly a fortnight after the fair, a ray of sunlight, penetrating through the window blind of his room, settled on Petrik's face.

"Draw the blind closer," said Anna Mikailovna to Velia; "I fear the light will be too much for him."

As the girl rose to comply with this request, she heard a faint whisper.

"No, do not; let it be as it is," said Petrik.

It was the first time he had spoken coherently since his delirium.

The two women bent over him joyfully.

"You hear me? I am with you," said the mother.

"Yes, I know." And then Petrik sank into a pensive silence, as if he were trying to collect his ideas.

"Oh, yes," he said at length in a scarcely audible voice; "how horrible it is."

Velia put her hand on his lips.

"Don't talk. The doctor said you were not to."

He pressed the hand to his lips and covered it with kisses. Tears flowed from his eyes; tears which he made no effort to restrain, for he felt that they were doing him good.

Just then Maxim entered the room, and though he walked softly, Petrik knew his uncle's step and turned his face to him.

"I have to thank you for a terrible lesson," he said; "a lesson I shall never forget. By enabling me to compare my lot with that of others you have shown me how selfish I have been, how fortunate I am, and how many blessings I possess. Please God, I shall never forget either the one or the other."

After this Petrik recovered rapidly, and in a few days rose from his bed.

He was greatly altered. His illness was the turning point of his life. So severe a shock, acting on so sensitive an organism, had wrought a radical change in his character. His dark despondency gave place to a tender pensiveness; the painfully anxious expression of his face to a look of tranquil content.

Maxim feared at first that this change was mainly due to a weakening of nervous activity, arising from his recent illness, and might not be lasting. But when month after month passed and Petrik remained always the same, never once either openly repining or showing by his manner that his mind was not at ease, the uncle saw that the revolution was permanent. The selfish contemplation of his own affliction, which had depressed his energies and warped the natural bent of his character, had been replaced by sympathy with the sorrows of others still more unfortunate. Sympathy had cured his sick soul of its morbid cravings, strengthening his moral sense, quickening his intelligence and giving him new ideals and a nobler purpose. He thought more of others and less of himself, and formed plans as well for his own future as for the benefit of his fellow-men. The half-broken soul was awakening from its long hibernation, like a young tree, half withered by the blasts of winter, on which spring has breathed its life-giving breeze.

CHAPTER XIX.

WHEN Petrik and Velia's engagement was made public and Velia informed her parents of her resolve to marry the blind young man from the manor, her mother had a good cry; but her father, after praying long before his ikons, said that he saw in it the will of God, and gave his consent; and as Anna Mikailovna loved Velia only less than her own son, and she and her husband desired above everything to see him united to one who possessed so many noble qualities, and was so likely to make him a devoted wife, they gladly gave their consent. Shortly afterwards the marriage was celebrated, and instead of going to the manor house nearly every day, Velia went there for good.

And then a new and great felicity began for Petrik. Nevertheless there were times when his very happiness seemed to breed misgiving and his mind was troubled with doubts. He felt that his happiness was greater than he deserved, and feared it would not last.

When told that he was likely to become a father, he received the news with a feeling akin to dismay.

But in all this there was none of the old egotism. He was too much concerned for his wife, too solicitous about her health, too apprehensive as to the future to become absorbed in fruitless introspection. Often, too, his thoughts went back to the terrible scene at the fair, and the sense of his own powerlessness to alleviate the sufferings of the unfortunates who were afflicted in like manner with himself, made him sad at heart.

* * * * *

In the same room where a generation before Petrik made his entrance into the world, there was again heard the plaintive cry of a new-born babe.

It was a fine healthy boy, and Velia recovered rapidly. Yet Petrik, instead of rejoicing as fathers generally do in like circumstances, seemed oppressed with the foreboding of some great calamity, and one day, the child being then about a week old, the young father was in a very agony of apprehension and suspense.

The surgeon had come to examine the child's eyes. Taking the little one in his arms, he carried it to the window, and drawing aside the curtain, let the light fall full on its face. Then he took out his instruments.

Meanwhile Petrik sat perfectly still, the very picture of wretchedness, and as heedless of the surgeon's proceedings, as if he had made up his mind to the worst.

"The child is sure to be blind," he moaned despairingly. "It had better never have been born."

Without answering, the surgeon went on deliberately with his examination. After a while he laid aside his ophthalmoscope and looked at Petrik with calm confidence.

"The pupil contracts. The child's eyes are normal; he can see," said the surgeon in a bold clear voice.

Petrik rose trembling. He must have heard the glad tidings which had just been pronounced; but, judging from his looks, he had as yet failed to grasp their significance. His shaking hands were laid on the window sill, he stood as if petrified, his face devoid of expression.

Up to that moment he had been in a state of excitement so intense as to be hardly conscious of his own existence; there were moments when his heart, after beating violently, appeared to stand still, and every nerve in his body thrilled with apprehension and dread. The darkness about him seemed concrete and palpable. It rushed on him like a visible enemy; and the sense of its reality was so vivid that he could scarce restrain himself from making a physical effort to shield his child from the flood of blackness which threatened to overwhelm him.

This was Petrik's state of mind while the surgeon was making his examination. Forebodings he had experienced before, but none so dark and hopeless. When apprehension reached the climax hope had disappeared. And then came the three blessed words:

"He can see.

Fear vanished; apprehension became hope; hope, certainty. His child could see. The revulsion produced a shock which flashed into his darkness like lightning in a sunless sky, conjuring up in his mind strange phantasms, and endowing him for a moment with unwonted powers. Whether they were sounds or sights he could not determine. But they were sounds which he could see. They sparkled like the sky vault, shone like the sun, waved like the rustling, whispering grass of the steppe.

These were the sensations of an instant. What followed he was unable to recall. But he affirmed that in this moment he saw Maxim, his mother and his wife.

Was it possible? Could it be that vague optical sensations, reaching the blind man's brain in a moment of ecstasy and through channels unknown to physiologists, had made their impress on his consciousness, like the shadowy negative of a photograph; that his sightless eyes had beheld the blue sky and the bright sun, the shining river, the breezy hillock where he had played as a child, and the three beings whom he best knew and most dearly loved?

Or were these phantasms merely the ghost-like reappearance, in Petrik's mental vision, of unknown streams and mountains, of trees waving over sunlit streams, of men and women once seen by unnumbered generations of forefathers?

Who can say?

He knew that the flash had come and gone, leaving him in the same darkness where he had dwelt from his birth. But the vision, whether imaginary or real, whether an illusion or a fact, had left its mark on his bright and radiant face. He stretched out his hands to his mother and Maxim with a gesture of joy.

"Oh, Petrik, what is the matter?" asked Anna Mikailovna, who was alarmed by the strangeness of her son's manner.

"Nothing. I seem to have seen you all. I am not sleeping, I suppose?"

"And now," asked the mother under her breath, "do you—will you be able to remember this time?"

Peter sighed deeply.

"No," he answered with an effort, "I fear not — and never again. But what matters it that I am blind? My boy can see."

His face resumed its wonted paleness, but it was still illumined with the same expression of exalted content.

CHAPTER XX.

A PUBLIC concert in the town of Kief.

It has been much talked about, and is the occasion of some excitement, due in part, let us hope, to the fact that the takings are to be handed over, without deduction, to a much deserving charitable institution; but the great attraction is undoubtedly the personality of the youthful performer.

He is young, rich, blind, and said to be a musical genius of the first order and a consummate pianist.

The room is crowded, the concert an assured pecuniary success before it has well begun.

As a young man, with a pale face and large beautiful eyes, comes forward every voice is hushed. But for their strange stillness and the fact that a simply-dressed fair young woman leads him by the hand nobody would have thought that those orbs had never seen.

"No wonder he makes such a sensation," observed

a scoffing on-looker to his neighbour. "His appearance is so dramatic; all arranged beforehand, I suppose."

In truth, Petrik's appearance was so striking as to raise great expectations among the audience, and predispose them to look for something *hors ligne*.

These expectations were amply fulfilled.

Southern Russians are passionately fond of music, and keenly appreciative of their national melodies. The audience, among whom were many not easily pleased, was completely, and from the first, carried away by Petrik's playing. A fresh and lively feeling for nature, a close and delicate sense of the beauties of Ruthenian music were revealed in the bold improvisations which flowed from the fingers of the blind musician. Rich in colour, sonorous and flexible, they rose now to the solemnity of a hymn; now burst forth into the passion and pathos of a song of love. Sometimes could be heard the spirit of the storm in the immensity of space, alternating with the voice of the wind, as it rustled quietly among the grass of the steppe, or blew wildly over a landscape white with snow.

When he paused an outburst of plaudits rang through the hall. The blind musician sat, according to his wont, with head slightly bent, listening to the unusual din. After waiting a few minutes he raised his hands, and in a moment the room was as silent as before.

Maxim looked at the audience, then at his nephew, with glistening, expectant and almost anxious eyes.

The old man listened with strained attention. He feared that these marvellous improvisations, flowing so freely from Petrik's soul, might be suddenly quenched as on some former occasions; that old memories and doubts, coming unbidden, might arrest his inspiration at its source and bring the performance to a painful close.

But Maxim was anxious without cause. Instead of growing weaker Petrik's playing becomes stronger and fuller. He held his audience spell-bound.

And the longer Maxim listens the more he seems to find in Petrik's playing something with which he is familiar, something which he had known before.

But suddenly Maxim's heart sinks again. A moment's pause, and the player strikes a note of deepest sadness. It fills the hall as with a moan, and then dies away in a plaintive wail.

To it straightway follows a melody so sweet, touching and pathetic that it brings the tears to every eye.

It is the cry of the blind beggars at the fair:

> "Give to the blind ones,
> Give to the blind ones,
> For Christ His sake."

The effect on the audience was so great that though, unlike Maxim, they had not heard the cry, and knew not the source of Petrik's inspiration, they kept silence for several minutes after he had finished —forgetting even to applaud.

" He has seen the light," murmured Maxim ; " he

has seen the light. There is no more room in his heart for selfish repinings; it is too full of sympathy for others. He has found his work and his mission. He will use the divine power which God has given him to plead the cause of the poor and oppressed, and help those who are less fortunate than himself."

As the old warrior thought this, his head sank on his breast. His work was done, and as the audience, recovering from the spell, broke into a very frenzy of applause, he had his reward; he felt that his life had not been spent in vain.

The blind musician had begun his career.

THE END.